BITTY BOPS

PreK Music Curriculum

Book 1: INFANTS: Ages Birth thru 1
Book 2: TODDLERS: Ages 2 thru 3
Book 3: PRESCHOOLERS: Ages 4 thru 5

David E. Knauss
Ph.D. in Music Education
Doc. Humane Letters

© 2016 David E. Knauss

Published by:
Music Excellence Publishing
deknauss@proton.me

BOOK 1: INFANTS: AGES BIRTH THRU 1
BOOK 2: TODDLERS: AGES 2 THRU 3
BOOK 3: PRESCHOOLERS: AGES 4 THRU 5

ISBN-13: 978-1-955820-00-4

First Printing, January, 2016

PRINTED IN THE UNITED STATES OF AMERICA

ALL RIGHTS RESERVED
No part of this publication may be reproduced, stored in a retrieval system, or transmitted in any form or by any means—for example, electronic, photocopy, recording—without the prior written permission of the publisher. The only exception is brief quotations in printed reviews.

DISCLAIMER
All the material contained in this book is provided for educational and informational purposes only. No responsibility can be taken for any results or outcomes resulting from the use of this material. While every attempt has been made to provide information that is both accurate and effective, the author does not assume any responsibility for the accuracy or use/misuse of this information.

Bitty Bops PreK Music Curriculum Books Overview

Research-based, Field-tested, and Comprehensive

These three bound-together *Bitty Bops* PreK Music Curriculum books (Infants, Toddlers, and Preschoolers) are research-based, field-tested, informal music instruction, and are inclusive of all the best current preschool music publications. *Bitty Bops* PreK Music Curriculum is unique in that **(1)** each lesson created by the music instructor is dove-tailed from activity to activity, providing appropriate scope and sequence, **(2)** the lessons are musically comprehensive (modally, rhythmically, metrically, stylistically) across an entire semester, and **(3)** all active music participations (listening, singing, chanting, moving, playing, performing, improvising, and creating) are included in each lesson.

Three completed example lesson plans (out of a possible 15 per semester) are provided in the Infants book to illustrate dove-tailing and lesson sequencing. This allows the music teacher to be artistically creative in completing the remaining 12 lessons for Infants. From the Infants three illustrated lessons, the same dove-tailing and sequencing is to be completed by the music teacher for Toddlers and Preschoolers. Open-ended lesson plans in this manner allow the music teacher to plan appropriate music activities to match the music development of the students.

Bitty Bops Music Curriculum is labeled PreK because these three bound-together books are the perfect informal music-building, music education foundation for leading into the formal music instruction Knauss K-12 Music Curriculum (Books 1, 1A, 2, 3, & 4). The Knauss K-12 Music Curriculum is available on Amazon.com, or through contacting Dr. Knauss at: deknauss@proton.me.

Bitty Bops Endorses the Following Publications

Feierabend, J., & Kahan, J. (2003). *The book of movement exploration: Can you move like this?* Chicago, IL: GIA Publications, Inc. ISBN 1-57999-264-1.

Feierabend, J. (2110). *First steps in classical music: Keeping the beat! (Compiled by John Feierabend)*. Chicago, IL: GIA Publications, Inc. CD#: CD-493.

Gordon, E.E. (2003). *A music learning theory for newborn and young children*. Chicago, IL: GIA Publications, Inc. ISBN: 1-57999-259-5.

Guilmartin, K.K. & Levinowitz, L.M. (2004, 2007). *Music together: Tambourine song collection*. Princeton, NJ: Music Together LLC. www.musictogether.com. (CD, 2007). CD#: MTTA13-CD.

Guilmartin, K.K. & Levinowitz, L.M. (2006, 2009). *Music together: Fiddle song collection*. Princeton, NJ: Music Together LLC. (CD, 2003). CD#: MTFI09-CD.

Guilmartin, K.K. & Levinowitz, L.M. (2003, 2006). *Music together: Triangle song collection*. Princeton, NJ: Music Together LLC. (CD, 2006). CD#: MTTR12-CD.

Guilmartin, K.K. & Levinowitz, L.M. (2007, 2010). *Music together: Drum song collection*. Princeton, NJ: Music Together LLC. (CD, 2012). CD#: MTDR13-CD.

Guilmartin, K.K. & Levinowitz, L.M. (2008). *Music together: Bongos song collection*. Princeton, NJ: Music Together LLC. (CD, 2005). CD#: MTBO11-CD.

Guilmartin, K.K. & Levinowitz, L.M. (2005, 2008). *Music together: Maracas song collection*. Princeton, NJ: Music Together LLC.

Guilmartin, K.K. & Levinowitz, L.M. (2009). *Music together: Bells song collection*. Princeton, NJ: Music Together LLC.

Guilmartin, K.K. & Levinowitz, L.M. (2010). *Music together: Sticks song collection*. Princeton, NJ: Music Together LLC. (CD, 2007). CD#: MTST11-CD.

Guilmartin, K.K. & Levinowitz, L.M. (2010). *Music together: Flute song collection*. Princeton, NJ: Music Together LLC.

Guilmartin, K.K. & Levinowitz, L.M. (2001). *Music together: Summer songs 1*. Princeton, NJ: Music Together LLC.

Guilmartin, K.K. & Levinowitz, L.M. (2007). *Music together: Summer songs 2*. Princeton, NJ: Music Together LLC.

Guilmartin, K.K. & Levinowitz, L.M. (2002). *Music together: Summer songs 3*. Princeton, NJ: Music Together LLC.

Guilmartin, K.K. & Levinowitz, L.M. (2002). *Music together: Babies*. Princeton, NJ: Music Together LLC.

Guilmartin, K.K. & Levinowitz, L.M. (2009). *Music together: Family favorites songbook for teachers: Bringing harmony home*. Princeton, NJ: Music Together LLC. ISBN: 978-0-615-32865-2.

Knauss, D. (2001). *Knauss K-12 music curriculum: Book 1A rhythm & tonal flash cards: Classroom (general) music for elementary and middle level: Supplement to book 1 (rev. ed. 2023)*. Kindle Direct Publishing: Amazon.com.

Nichol, Doug (1975). *A Nichol's worth. Volumes 1 & 2 (1975). Volumes 3 & 4 (1978).* Buffalo, NY: Tometic Associates LTD. Reprinted with permission. University Park, PA: The Pennsylvania State University Bookstore.

Valerio, W., Reynolds, A., Bolton, B., Taggart, C., & Gordon, E. (2000). *Music play: Book 1: The early childhood music curriculum guide for parents, teachers and caregivers*. Chicago, IL: GIA Publications, Inc. Item #G-J236. ISBN: 1-57999-027-4.

Basic Set Up

Working with a Budget. If you are just beginning a preschooler music program and working with a beginning budget, it is not advisable to purchase all of the listed publications and CDs because there is a certain amount of crossover from publication to publication. Check carefully the index lists in this curriculum for choosing which publications you prefer to purchase first.

Music on the Internet. Many of the songs listed in *Bitty Bops* PreK Music Curriculum indices may be found on the Internet, both in "pdf" written music and in "mp3" recorded music, free of charge or minimal charge.

Materials and Instruments. Inexpensive sheer nylon scarves and a small set of inexpensive hand percussion instruments may suffice for the beginning year or two. Scarves may be purchased from a superstore (such as Walmart, Big Lots, Target, etc.). Inexpensive instruments in toy-quality may also be purchased from a superstore, and then later replaced with instrument-quality from any number of online music instrument distributors (such as West Music Company, Latin Percussion, Staggs, etc.).

Informal vs. Formal Music Education

***Bitty Bops* PreK Music Education Curriculum** (Books 1-2-3: Infants, Toddlers, Preschoolers: Ages birth through Kindergarten) is designed for informal instruction, much like what happens in a preschool academy or childcare setting of learning through play. Informal instruction is based on learning through play; whereas, formal instruction is learning through focused schoolwork.

Informal Instruction
- ♪ Instruction resembles play
- ♪ Child may or may not participate
- ♪ Child often does not appear to be attentive
- ♪ Instructor should give the child a silent space after each musical event for child's possible response, but should never correct any response, nor show any negative if the child gives no response
- ♪ If the child gives a response, the instructor should mimic that response, acknowledging the importance of the child's own musical participation
- ♪ When a child gives a response, a musical conversation often evolves, initiated by the child

♪ Instruction is best when it is part of the child's everyday life

Knauss K-12 Music Education Curriculum (Books 1-1A-2-3-4: Kindergarten through Grade 12) is designed for superior formal instruction. Formal instruction works well in public, parochial, homeschool, or any kind of group instructional settings beyond PreKindergarten. (Available on Amazon.com)

Formal Instruction
♪ Instruction that happens in K-12 public school settings
♪ Instructor is the model, and a musical response is expected from the children
♪ The instructor should not sing or chant with the children
♪ Children need to learn to be independent of the instructor, and the instructor needs to be listening to the children's responses in order to provide appropriate feedback and/or correction

Both Informal and Formal Instruction
♪ Important for the child to be immersed in a rich musical environment
♪ A variety of songs with or without words in a variety of styles
♪ A variety of recorded selections in a variety of styles

Beyond General Music Education

Beyond general music education, in the much-neglected Spiritual realm, **Let's All Praise: As It Is In Heaven** (Books 1-1A-2-3-4) curriculum series is for teaching kids to be worshippers and musician-warriors with perfected praises as Jesus said (Matthew 21:15-16, NKJV; Psalm 8:2, NIV; Psalm 149, KJV). We are lovers of God and His children who want only the best world for our kids. And we know kids are God's best workers. Here is a curriculum with everything you need to know about the power of Spiritual music for building God's Kingdom and our world—music activities as easy as counting to 4 and knowing the first 7 letters of the alphabet. (Available on Amazon.com)

Book 1: Curriculum Lessons = Teacher's Manual for 10 Scriptural-Spiritual lessons on God's music from Genesis to Revelation.
Book 1A: Curriculum Lessons Student Workbook = Student Workbook for Book 1 for students to have the music verses with them for their entire ministry lives.
Book 2: Music, Movement, and Colors = Teacher's Manual for music arrangements, including student charts for lyrics and instrumental parts, praise flagging movements, and praise flagging colors.
Book 3: Bonus Narrative = Narrative Text of 20 chapters (like bonus DVDs in a movie set) reveal the hidden Scripture meanings of what this is all about.
Book 4: Praise With Harps = Self-Teaching Harp Manual for beginners to praise the Lord with harps, join the ongoing activities of His Throne Room, and extend His Throne Room boundaries "on earth as it is in Heaven." Sequenced easy harp arrangements may also be used as accompaniments to the music in Books 1 & 2.

Bitty Bops Documents for Infants, Toddlers, and Preschoolers

BOOK 1: INFANTS	BOOK 2: TODDLERS	BOOK 3: PRESCHOOLERS
Doc 00: How to Use *Bitty Bops—Infants* PreK Music Curriculum (p. 2)	**Doc 10:** How to Use *Bitty Bops—Toddlers* PreK Music Curriculum (p. 62)	**Doc 20:** How to Use *Bitty Bops—Preschoolers* PreK Music Curriculum (p. 120)
Doc 01: Infants Lesson Plan Structure and Activities Explained (p. 5)	**Doc 11:** Toddlers Lesson Plan Structure and Activities Explained (p. 65)	**Doc 21:** Preschoolers Lesson Plan Structure and Activities Explained (p. 123)
Doc 02: How Infants Learn Music (p. 7)	**Doc 12:** How Toddlers Learn Music (p. 67)	**Doc 22:** How Preschoolers Learn Music (p. 125)
Doc 03: Infants Music Lesson Plans (p. 11)	**Doc 13:** Toddlers Music Lesson Plans (p. 70)	**Doc 23:** Preschoolers Music Lesson Plans (p. 128)
Doc 04: Infants Songs Notebook Index (p. 20)	**Doc 14:** Toddlers Songs Notebook Index (p. 79)	**Doc 24:** Preschoolers Songs Notebook Index (p. 137)
Doc 05: Infants Music Together Books Index (p. 30)	**Doc 15:** Toddlers Music Together Books Index (p. 88)	**Doc 25:** Preschoolers Music Together Books Index (p. 158)
Doc 06: Infants Music Play Book Index (p. 45)	**Doc 16:** Toddlers Music Play Book Index (p. 103)	**Doc 26:** Preschoolers Music Play Book Index (p. 173)
Doc 07: Infants Nichol's Worth Books Index (p. 49)	**Doc 17:** Toddlers Nichol's Worth Books Index (p. 107)	**Doc 27:** Preschoolers Nichol's Worth Books Index (p. 177)
Doc 08: Infants Movement Exploration and Keeping the Beat Index (p. 54)	**Doc 18:** Toddlers Movement Exploration and Keeping the Beat Index (p. 112)	**Doc 28:** Preschoolers Movement Exploration and Keeping the Beat Index (p. 182)

About the Author

Dr. David E. Knauss taught inner-city K-12 general music for 3 decades, helped to develop an award-winning music department and K-12 general music curriculum [*Knauss K-12 General Music Curriculum*], led his students to relate to each other as family members and become outstanding musicians, and saw the community's artist values change as the departmental music program became the city's icon. While studying at Penn State University, Dr. Knauss added to his teaching experiences preschool music from birth through kindergarten [*Bitty Bops PreK Music Curriculum*]. As an adjunct music professor for nearly a decade, Dr. Knauss taught undergraduate and graduate music education methods, music education philosophy, and master classes to classroom (general) music teachers and primary school teachers. Dr. Knauss has now written a Biblical curriculum [*Let's All Praise: As It Is In Heaven*] and Dr. and Mrs. Knauss teach youngsters of all ages to be warrior-musicians for building God's Kingdom and our world (Psalm 8:2, NIV; Psalm 149:1-9, NKJV).

"In a lifelong search for my students' learning limits, I only ever found my teaching limits! Every time I overcame my limits, the students were right with me." —D. Knauss

Music Education Support

Feel free to email Dr. Knauss at any time, as often as you like (knaussde@gmail.com), with any questions concerning teaching music education. Dr. Knauss freely mentors music education excellence to successive generations.

Dr. David E. and Mrs. Joanne L. Knauss
Doctor of Philosophy in Music Education, Penn State University
Doctor of Humane Letters, The Wesley Synod International, Canterbury, England

BITTY BOPS

BOOK 1: INFANTS
PreK Music Curriculum
for
Ages Birth thru 1

How To Use *Bitty Bops—Infants* Music Curriculum

There are four main sections to *Bitty Bops—Infants* Music Curriculum.

INFANTS LESSON STRUCTURE & ACTIVITIES EXPLAINED
(1) *Bitty Bops—Infants* music teachers must first learn the Infant Lesson Structure and explanation of Infant Activities. **(See Document 01 and paragraphs in Document 04.)**

HOW INFANTS LEARN MUSIC
(2) Dr. Edwin Gordon's research and publication explain how pre-K12 children learn, their responses, and how a teacher should interact with the student for each of the stages of:
> ACCULTURATION (Infants: Birth to Age 2-4)
> IMITATION (Toddlers: Ages 2-4 to 3-5)
> ASSIMILATION (Preschoolers: Ages 3-5 to 4-6)

All levels of *Bitty Bops* music teachers need to know what comprises these stages, how to recognize children's responses for each level, and how the *Bitty Bops* music teacher should interact rhythmically and tonally with the children on each level. For this level, *Bitty Bops—Infants*, music teachers especially need to know the stages of ACCULTURATION (Infants: Birth to Age 2-4). **(See Document 02.)**

COMPILATION OF CURRICULAR MATERIALS
(3) *Bitty Bops—Infants* music teachers should be thoroughly familiar with all the songs and activities so that Infants may be taught according to their developmental and response stages.
> INFANT SONGS COLLECTION: These categorical songs and activities, indexed by music activity categories, are compiled and field-tested by an experienced pre-K12 music teacher for more than a decade of teaching at this age level. **(See Document 04.)**
> MUSIC TOGETHER SONG COLLECTIONS: From Ken Guilmartin and Dr. Lillian Levinowitz, pre-K12 music experts at Rowan University. **(See Document 05.)**
>> Tambourine Song Collection
>> Fiddle Song Collection
>> Triangle Song Collection
>> Drum Song Collection
>> Bongos Song Collection
>> Maracas Song Collection
>> Bells Song Collection
>> Sticks Song Collection
>> Flute Song Collection
>> Summer Songs 1
>> Summer Songs 2
>> Summer Songs 3
>> Babies
>> Family Favorites Songbook for Teachers
>
> MUSIC PLAY: BOOK 1: From Dr. Gordon and his associates at Temple University and surrounding areas, this music book is created based on the music learning sequence Gordon research for pre-K12ers. **(See Document 06.)**

NICHOL'S WORTH: VOLUMES 1-2-3-4: A great collection of fun and humorous songs. These are witty, folk-like songs in four volumes, featuring all combinations of Meters (duple, triple, and multi-metric combined); Modes (Major, Minor, Dorian, Mixolydian, Phrygian, Lydian, and multi-tonal); in vocal textures (unison, combinable songs, partner songs, ostinatos, countermelodies, and rounds) that many other song collections neglect to include. **(See Document 07.)** (For the much-neglected Locrian mode, see the Knauss Music Curriculum, Book 1, pp. 50, 82-84. All modes may be sung in canon, see Knauss Music Curriculum, Book 3, pp. 18-20. For the Locrian mode, transpose the canon to the scale notes B to B: Ti-Do-Re-Mi-Fa-So-La-Ti.)

THE BOOK OF MOVEMENT EXPLORATION: CAN YOU MOVE LIKE THIS? Dr. John Feierabend has many years of research and experience with pre-K12 music teaching as well as expertly certified in the Kódaly music education approach. **(See Document 08.)**

FIRST STEPS IN CLASSICAL MUSIC: KEEPING THE BEAT! Dr. John Feierabend compiled an accompanying CD to the above book featuring many great classical works for children's exposure to classical styles. **(See Document 08.)**

INFANTS MUSIC LESSON PLANS

(4) *Bitty Bops—Infants* music teachers need to be familiar with all of the above information, songs, and activities, to the point of having them memorized so that they naturally flow out of the music teacher in smooth, well-transitioned, dove-tailed music lessons. See the lesson plan instructions and example music lesson plans for dovetailing and planning a balanced presentation and exposure to all Active Participations, Rhythm and Tonal Patterns, Song Categories, Meters, and Modes. **(See Document 03.)**

Contents for *Bitty Bops—Infants*
(Documents 00-08)

Page

Document 00: How to Use *Bitty Bops—Infants* Music Curriculum 2

Document 01: Infants Lesson Structure and Activities Explained 5

Document 02: How Infants Learn Music 7

Document 03: Infants Music Lesson Plans 11

Document 04: Infants Songs Notebook Index 20

Document 05: Infants Music Together Books Index 30

Document 06: Infants Music Play Book Index 45

Document 07: Infants Nichol's Worth Books Index 49

Document 08: Infants Movement Exploration and Keeping the Beat Index 54

Infants Classes & Activities Explained
Birth thru 1

"Cardinal" Rules that must never be broken or neglected when teaching pre-K12 music classes:

1. Every song must have movement on the steady beat (except for purposeful interpretive movements). Always plan your movements. Also, copy any students' spontaneous movements.
2. All movements must exhibit a steady beat.
3. Male and female teachers alike must use their head voices so that the students learn to match in their light head voices. When all students are securely in tune, then the male teacher may use his lower voice and be certain that the students are aware of the octave transfer.
4. The teacher should never play an instrument to have students match pitches, because the transfer gap in timbre from instrument to voice is too wide. The teacher must always use voice to voice.
5. At the end of every singing song, the teacher sings the "Sol-Do" of the song with hand motions—palms pointing down at chest level (Sol) and ending on the floor or waist level (Do). Pause for two seconds after the Sol, to allow for students to respond if they wish with the Do.

Each Infants Lesson Plan should contain the following, depending on class length:

1. Bouncing or lap song
2. Finger play / body awareness songs and activities
3. Large gross motor activity / traveling movement—if class is mostly mobile infants
4. Steady beat activities to utilize each of the following instruments—(drums, shakers, sticks)
5. Peek-a-boo song with scarves
6. Rocking song
7. Rhythmic and tonal patterns, both simple and complex
8. Group dance activity
9. From one music activity to the next, music concepts dovetailed (see Lesson Plan chart).
10. For the music learning stages of infants, see ACCULTURATION stages in the chart of How Infants Learn Music (see Document 02).
11. Each class should contain approximately 12-14 songs including hello and goodbye songs, dependent on time length of class. The use of the word parent in the follow paragraphs denotes caregiver, babysitter, family relative, or anyone who regularly brings the infant to each class.

Repetition. Repetition the most important aspect of learning in early childhood music. Songs are repeated from week to week, but varied with different instruments and movements. The majority of each class is repeated familiar songs and activities, with only a few being introduced as new. When new ones are consistently repeated, they too become familiar.

Actions Not Explanations. The teacher begins each class with singing, ends with singing, and even sings all 4-word-or-less instructions between activities (only if instructions are absolutely needed). In preschool ages, children do not learn with linguistic explanations—they learn experientially. Only parents need explanations, such as the preschool stages of learning (see ACCULTURATION stages in chart of How Infants Learn Music (see Document 02), or reminders why their participation is the superior modeling for their infant. When parents need explanations or reminders that they are active participants all the time, provide these apart from the flow of the lesson. Parents should sing every song the same as the teacher, because infants need the emotional connection of the parent voice that they have been listening to since before they were born. Music is learned in the same way as language (Suzuki's "mother tongue" concept). So it is because we speak to infants, regardless of their ability to answer or understand, to immerse them in unlimited exposure. In this way, infants will acquire the sounds and rhythms. It is only later in Kindergarten or after that they should be asked to read and write in the language.

Smooth Transitions. When moving from song to song, either sing a transition melodic phrase, or a clean-up song. Do not speak instructions. Keep the music ongoing. Think about what is coming next and prepare infants and parents for the activity with movement to do together. "March with me," or "caw like a crow," or just jump right into the next song or activity. Don't stop the music, but rather keep songs flowing from one to the next. If a child does not want to "clean up," they will eventually copy the others. When you, the teacher, give out the next object for the next activity, you can trade them objects without saying a word or bringing attention to their negative behavior. In this way, always promote a positive atmosphere.

Playing Not Performing. Real learning that will stick, will happen when infants feel comfortable in their learning environment, when there is repetition, and when they are emotionally connected to the activity through laughter and enjoyment. Growing a relationship with that infant can happen through music class, which of course is inherently fun, but a child will also naturally gravitate to someone who will "play" with them. An effective early childhood teacher is one who has a playful spirit and is thoroughly animated. Children learn through play and are naturally playful beings. They will respond to adults who are authentically silly right along with them. Teachers need to find that playful spirit that feels natural to them.

Acceptance Without Expectations. Children are different learners. Some are active participants and some do not participate at all but they are absorbing the class and its activities like a sponge, regardless of what they are doing on the exterior. What they do in class, most likely they will imitate at home where they are most comfortable. We take the children, where they are, and whatever type of learner they are, and accept them as they are. Early childhood music education, informal music education, is not at all like formal music education in K-12, where responses are expected. The teacher must be aware that participation or responses may or may not happen depending on the learning stage of the infant (see ACCULTURATION stages in chart of How Infants Learn Music (see Document 02).

Parent Participation. Parents should be reminded that they are to be their infant's example. Parents must be involved, not sitting or standing as silent observers outside the activity circle. Infants need to see that their parents value music and that they lead by modeling, showing the joy of music even when the infant is not participating. Parent socializing should not happen during class, and should be addressed either through an initial handout explaining class procedure and parental expectations, or verbal reminders. Remind the parents to turn their "talking" voices off as they enter the room. Parents may also need to be reminded that the music curriculum is developmentally geared to the infant child so repetition is a key component. Infants are emotionally connected to their parents and their voices, so when modeling, remind parents that it doesn't matter how well or perfectly they sound. It is primarily the fact that it is THEIR sound their infant will respond to and connect with. This ensures that the best learning will happen!

How Infants Learn Music

Gordon, E.E. (2003). *A music learning theory for newborn and young children*. Chicago, IL: GIA Publications, Inc. ISBN: 1-57999-259-5.

"Audiation takes place when one hears and comprehends music silently, the sound of the music no longer being or never having been physically present. In contrast, aural perception takes place when one hears music when its sound is physically present." (p. 25).

"Audition is to music what thought is to language. Audiating while you are performing music is like thinking while you are speaking, and audiating while listening to music is like thinking about what persons have said and are saying as you are listening to them speak." (p. 25).

"Audiation is the basis of music aptitude." (p. 25).

Music learning sequentially begins for Birth to Age 2-4 with ACCULTURATION stages. (See the following ACCULTURATION stages.)

TYPES	CHILD'S RESPONSES	TEACHER'S INTERACTION
1. ACCULTURATION: Birth to age 2-4: participates with little consciousness of the environment (p. 41) ACCULTURATION begins before birth in the womb and continues after birth when children begin to become musically acculturated in various ways. They may hear their parents, sisters, brothers, and other children sing and chant. They may hear music performed in the home. They may hear musicians in live performance on TV or in concert. They begin to distinguish sounds in their environment from the vocal sounds that they themselves produce. They learn to discriminate similarities and differences among sounds in their environment. As this process unfolds, they begin to change from being only hearers of sounds to being participants in the making of musical sounds. Acculturation has three sub stages of development: (a) young children respond to their environment by listening, (b) children make babble sounds and movements that are not particularly related to the environment, and (c)	1.A. ABSORPTION: Hears and aurally collects the sounds of music in the environment (p. 41) Children respond to their environment by listening. (p. 43) CHILD'S RESPONSES OR REACTIONS TO MUSIC: Child turns his/her head, or looks toward music, or even watches while hearing the music; but does not make a vocal response. Child sometimes will move during the silences.	TEACHER'S INTERACTION WITH CHILD'S RESPONSES: Sing 3-note, diatonic, tonal Acculturation patterns while making eye contact with individual children and smiling (neutral syllable "bum.") Chant rhythm Acculturation patterns while making eye contact with individual children and smiling (neutral syllable "ba.") Model a deep, full breath preceding each tonal pattern. Model a deep, full macro beat breath preceding each rhythm pattern. During tonal pattern guidance, invite a second adult to breathe and echo your diatonic tonal pattern. Do not verbally or physically encourage child to make a response. Be sensitive to child by not continuing pattern guidance too long. Continue with unstructured, informal guidance during tonal and rhythm Acculturation pattern guidance and classroom activities. Continue singing tonal Acculturation patterns and performing music in a variety of tonalities and meters while moving with continuous flow. Observe indications of the variations among each child's personal tempo with rhythm patterns.

TYPES	CHILD'S RESPONSES	TEACHER'S INTERACTION
children make music babble sounds and movements in response to the environment.	1.B. RANDOM RESPONSE: Moves and babbles in response to, but without relation to, the sounds of music in the environment (p. 41) Children make babble sounds and movements that are not particularly related to the environment. (p. 43) CHILD'S RESPONSES OR REACTIONS TO MUSIC: Child begins to participate by babbling sounds and movements that are not coordinated, and with vocal responses that do not resemble the singing in his/her environment. Child may also perform various movements that seem to be stimulated by, but not necessarily related to, his/her environment.	TEACHER'S INTERACTION WITH CHILD'S RESPONSES: Continue with all previous suggestions in 1.A. Reinforce vocal sounds and movements that young children perform. If a child responds with what you determine to be his/her personal pitch, turn that pitch into the dominant or tonic of your song and patterns temporarily. Then, perform the same tonal pattern in the original keyality in which you presented the song. Continue chanting rhythm Acculturation patterns and performing music in a variety of tonalities and meters while moving with continuous flow. Continue to model a deep, full macro beat breath preceding each rhythm pattern.

TYPES	CHILD'S RESPONSES	TEACHER'S INTERACTION
	1.C. PURPOSEFUL RESPONSE: Tries to relate movement and babble to the sounds of music in the environment (p. 41) Children make babble sounds and movements in response to the environment. (p. 43) **CHILD'S RESPONSES OR REACTIONS TO MUSIC:** Child vocalizes a response that is related to the music in his/her environment. Child will be responding with a singing voice quality. The response may be characteristic of his/her personal pitch, or may correspond to the tonality presented, such as the resting tone or the dominant pitch. Child may attempt the adult's tonal or rhythm pattern, or his/her own pattern, but not necessarily with an accurate or precise performance.	**TEACHER'S INTERACTION WITH CHILD'S RESPONSES:** Introduce structured, informal guidance during tonal and rhythm Acculturation pattern guidance and classroom activities. Continue all previous suggestions in 1.A. Imitate child's vocal responses and continue to sing tonal Acculturation patterns. Be alert for child's spontaneous performances of a resting tone or dominant pitch, either on its own or within a pattern, which signals you to begin singing perfect 5th and perfect 4th tonal Imitation patterns to that child. After a child performs a resting tone or dominant pitch, do not drill and practice in expectation that the child will precisely imitate an Acculturation pattern. Encourage spontaneous songs, chants, and movements created by child. Continue singing tonal and rhythm Acculturation patterns and performing music in a variety of tonalities and meters while moving with continuous flow.

Gordon, E.E. (2003). *A music learning theory for newborn and young children*. Chicago, IL: GIA Publications, Inc. ISBN: 1-57999-259-5. (summarized from pp. 41, 43).

Infants Music Lesson Plans
Guidelines for Planning

(1) Whatever you choose as the "Hello Song" and "Goodbye Song" for the first class of the semester, keep those songs consistent for the whole semester. Change the "Hello" and "Goodbye" songs to different ones only in a following semester.

(2) Follow careful Dovetailing of Modes and Meters from activity to activity so that something remains familiar from activity to activity in each lesson—thus controlling the number of music concepts that are familiar vs. new from activity to activity. Also carefully track the repetition and changing of active participations ("ing" words) down the column. (See the circled items for how they are repeated or "dovetailed" from activity to activity.)

(3) Carefully plan the number of familiar activities, as opposed to new activities, from lesson to lesson. Repeat a majority of familiar from the previous lesson(s) and use a small number of new. (The arrows that point forward into the next lesson plan indicate the songs that are carried as familiar over into the next lesson plan.)

(4) As much as possible, be sure to include each of the Active Participations of Singing, Chanting, Moving, Playing, Performing, Creating, and Improvising in some way throughout the progress of each lesson. (See the third column labeled Dovetailing of Mode / Meter / Specialty.)

(5) Choose 3-4 Duple and Triple Rhythms and insert into the Lesson Plan where appropriate. Choose 3-4 Tonal Patterns and insert into the Lesson Plan where appropriate. Chant on neutral syllable "ba" for rhythm and sing on neutral syllable "nu" or "loo" for tonal. Perform the rhythm and tonal patterns looking directly into infants' faces. Pause a second or two after each to give infant time to respond if (s)he desires. Whatever response given, immediately copy it back to the infant and give a response moment. (These rhythms and tonal patterns are found in the Knauss Music Curriculum, Book 1A.)

(6) Plan for music activities that are at the Infant's level as well as music that is beyond the Infant's level, the same as parents babble single words or "baby talk" to their infants, as well as speak adult-level coherent paragraphs with complex words and sentence structures, even second languages.

(7) Include listening, moving, and playing with an instrumental selection in each lesson—whether popular, classical, cultural, or whatever.

(8) Because music potential is genius level at birth, and slowly declines from there, always provide the infants with the greatest exposure to all kinds and levels and complexity of music—nothing is outside their exposure and absorption abilities at this age.

Tracking the Content of Infants Lesson Plans

When planning the sequence of each next lesson from the one before, the goal is for an evenly varied musical exposure and experience across each class semester.

	Active Participations				Rhythm & Tonal Patterns			Songs								Meters			Modes						
	\					\		Song Categories							Meters			Modes						
	Singing / Chanting	Moving	Playing / Performing	Creating / Improvising	Duple Rhythm Patterns	Triple Rhythm Patterns	Tonal Patterns	Bouncing Song / Lap Song	Finger Play / Body Awareness	Peek-a-Boo Song	Steady Beat Activity with Instruments	Dancing Song	Rocking Song	Large Gross Motor Activity with Movement	Duple Meter	Triple Meter	Unusual Meter	Major (Ionian)	Minor (Aeolian)	Mixolydian	Dorian	Lydian	Phrygian	Locrian
Lesson 1																								
Lesson 2																								
Lesson 3																								
Lesson 4																								
Lesson 5																								
Lesson 6																								
Lesson 7																								
Lesson 8																								
Lesson 9																								
Lesson 10																								
Lesson 11																								
Lesson 12																								
Lesson 13																								
Lesson 14																								
Lesson 15																								
TOTALS (Goal is for an evenly varied musical exposure and experience across each class semester)																								

Infants Music Lesson Plan 1

Choose 3-4 Duple and Triple Rhythms and insert into the Lesson Plan where appropriate.
Choose 3-4 Major and Minor Tonal Patterns and insert into the Lesson Plan where appropriate.

CATEGORY	MATERIALS	DOVETAILING OF MODE / METER / SPECIALTY	ACTIVITY
Hello Song	"Hello Song" Music Together—Sticks Song Collection, p. 13	Major / Duple Singing & Pat / Clap the Duple Meter	Sit in a circle and sway back and forth gently on the macrobeats—sing close to each baby so (s)he can focus on your mouth
Bouncing Song / Lap Song	"Dance to Your Daddy" Music Together—Flute Song Collection, p. 35	Minor / Duple Singing	Bounce babies in one of the ways as shown in the 4 pictures. Change bounce to another picture when the song repeats
Finger Play / Body Awareness	"Pussy-Cat, Pussy-Cat" (Mother Goose Club), Infant Collection, p. 20	Minor / Triple Singing	Using your fingers, lightly tap the triple microbeats on infant. Do a tickle at the end of the song
Peek-a-Boo Song	"Round and Round the Haystack" Infant Collection, p. 21	Triple Chanting	Cover mommy or daddy or infant with a shear scarf and follow the stepping and uncovering directions while chanting
Steady Beat Activity with Instruments	"Pat-a-Cake Pat-a-Cake" Infant Collection, p. 22	Major / Triple Singing & Playing (sometimes adapted to Minor)	Play on the dotted quarter macrobeats with all kinds of percussion instruments while singing
Dancing Song	"Tingalayo" Music Together—Tambourine Song Collection, p. 18	Major / Duple Singing & Dancing & Marching	March and dance with scarves while singing
Rocking Song	"Bim Bam" Music Together—Maracas Song Collection, p. 22	Minor / Duple Singing & Playing	Rock while singing and playing—use various kinds of instruments to play either the macrobeats or microbeats
Large Gross Motor Activity with Traveling Movement	"Ladybug" Music Together—Triangle Song Collection, p. 19	Minor / Triple Singing & (Dorian Moving implied)	Sing and move the song changing the words to lots of different animals that cause the infants to employ large traveling movements
Goodbye Song	"Goodbye, So Long, Farewell" by Ken Guilmartin Music Together—Sticks Song Collection, p. 45	Major / Triple Swaying & Pat / Clap / Clap the Triple Meter	Back to sitting in a circle—use each of the infant's and parent's names to sing goodbye—sway a goodbye hand to the triple meter

(There are only 9 activities above; 12-14 are to be planned by repeating categories.)

Infants Music Lesson Plan 2

Choose 3-4 Duple and Triple Rhythms and insert into the Lesson Plan where appropriate.
Choose 3-4 Major and Minor Tonal Patterns and insert into the Lesson Plan where appropriate.

CATEGORY	MATERIALS	DOVETAILING OF MODE / METER / SPECIALTY	ACTIVITY
Hello Song	"Hello Song" Music Together—Sticks Song Collection, p. 13	Major (Duple) Singing & Pat / Clap the Duple Meter	Sit in a circle and sway back and forth gently on the macrobeats—sing close to each baby so (s)he can focus on your mouth
Bouncing Song / Lap Song	"The Grasshopper and the Elephant" A Nichol's Worth, Vol. 1, p. 9	(Phrygian) (Duple) Singing	Bounce babies on thighs, on knees, or gently in the air. Choose one way for the grasshopper and another for the elephant
Finger Play / Body Awareness	"Pussy-Cat, Pussy-Cat" (Mother Goose Club), Infant Collection, p. 20: Perform Minor Tonal Patterns	(Minor) (Triple) Singing	Using your fingers, lightly tap the triple microbeats on infant. Do a tickle at the end of the song
Peek-a-Boo Song	"Round and Round the Haystack" Infant Collection, p. 21: Perform Triple Rhythm Patterns	(Triple) Chanting	Cover mommy or daddy or infant with a shear scarf and follow the stepping and uncovering directions while chanting
Steady Beat Activity with Instruments	"Water Music: Allegro: (Gigue)" G.F. Handel Track 14, First Steps in Classical Music CD-493: Major Tonal Patterns	(Major) (Duple Compound) Listening & Playing	Perform the beat with all kinds of available percussion instruments
Dancing Song	"Tingalayo" Music Together—Tambourine Song Collection, p. 18	(Major) (Duple) Singing & Dancing & Marching	March and dance with scarves while singing
Rocking Song	"Bim Bam" Music Together—Maracas Song Collection, p. 22: Perform Duple Rhythm Patterns	(Minor) (Duple) Singing & Playing	Rock while singing and playing—use various kinds of instruments to play either the macrobeats or microbeats
Large Gross Motor Activity w/ Traveling Movement	"Ladybug" Music Together—Triangle Song Collection, p. 19	(Minor) (Triple) Singing & Moving	Sing and move the song changing the words to lots of different animals that cause the infants to employ large traveling movements
Goodbye Song	"Goodbye, So Long, Farewell" by Ken Guilmartin: Music Together—Sticks, p. 45	Major (Triple) Swaying & Pat / Clap / Clap the Triple Meter	Back to sitting in a circle—use each of the infant's and parent's names to sing goodbye—sway a goodbye hand to the triple meter

(There are only 9 activities above; 12-14 are to be planned by repeating categories.)

Infants Music Lesson Plan 3

Choose 3-4 Duple and Triple Rhythms and insert into the Lesson Plan where appropriate.
Choose 3-4 Major and Minor Tonal Patterns and insert into the Lesson Plan where appropriate.

CATEGORY	MATERIALS	DOVETAILING OF MODE / METER / SPECIALTY	ACTIVITY
Hello Song	"Hello Song" Music Together—Sticks Song Collection, p. 13	Major (Duple) Singing & Pat / Clap the Duple Meter	Sit in a circle and sway back and forth gently on the macrobeats—sing close to each baby so (s)he can focus on your mouth
Bouncing Song / Lap Song	"The Grasshopper and the Elephant" A Nichol's Worth, Vol. 1, p. 9	(Phrygian) (Duple) Singing	Bounce babies on thighs, on knees, or gently in the air. Choose one way for the grasshopper and another for the elephant
Finger Play / Body Awareness	"Pussy-Cat, Pussy-Cat" (Mother Goose Club), Infant Collection, p. 20 Perform Minor Tonal Patterns	(Minor) Triple Singing	Using your fingers, lightly tap the triple microbeats on infant. Do a tickle at the end of the song
Peek-a-Boo Song	"Sneak and Peek" Music Together—Drum Song Collection, p. 20	(Dorian) (Duple) Chanting	Cover mommy or daddy or infant with a shear scarf and follow the stepping and uncovering directions while chanting
Steady Beat Activity with Instruments	"Water Music: Allegro: (Gigue)" G.F. Handel Track 14, First Steps in Classical Music CD-493: Major Tonal Patterns	(Major) (Duple Compound) Listening & Playing	Perform the beat with all kinds of available percussion instruments
Dancing Song	"Tingalayo" Music Together—Tambourine Song Collection, p. 18	(Major) (Duple) Singing & Dancing & Marching	March and dance with scarves while singing
Rocking Song	"Bim Bam" Music Together—Maracas Song Collection, p. 22: Perform Duple Rhythm Patterns	(Minor) (Duple) Singing & Playing	Rock while singing and playing—use various kinds of instruments to play either the macrobeats or microbeats
Large Gross Motor Activity with Traveling Movement	"Drummers Marching" Music Together—Triangle Song Collection, p. 42: Perform Triple Rhythm Patterns	(Minor) (Triple) Singing & Moving	(Follow the directions for Infants) March index and third finger up and down infant
Goodbye Song	"Goodbye, So Long, Farewell" by Ken Guilmartin Music Together—Sticks, p. 45	Major (Triple) Swaying & Pat / Clap / Clap the Triple Meter	Back to sitting in a circle—use each of the infant's and parent's names to sing goodbye—sway a goodbye hand to the triple meter

(There are only 9 activities above; 12-14 are to be planned by repeating categories.)

Infants Music Lesson Plan 4

Choose 3-4 Duple and Triple Rhythms and insert into the Lesson Plan where appropriate.
Choose 3-4 Major and Minor Tonal Patterns and insert into the Lesson Plan where appropriate.

CATEGORY	MATERIALS	DOVETAILING OF MODE / METER / SPECIALTY	ACTIVITY
Hello Song	"Hello Song" Music Together—Sticks Song Collection, p. 13	Major Duple Singing & Pat / Clap the Duple Meter	Sit in a circle and sway back and forth gently on the macrobeats—sing close to each baby so (s)he can focus on your mouth
Bouncing Song / Lap Song			
Finger Play / Body Awareness			
Peek-a-Boo Song			
Steady Beat Activity with Instruments			
Dancing Song			
Rocking Song			
Large Gross Motor Activity with Traveling Movement			
Goodbye Song	"Goodbye, So Long, Farewell" by Ken Guilmartin Music Together—Sticks, p. 45	Major Triple Swaying & Pat / Clap / Clap the Triple Meter	Back to sitting in a circle—use each of the infant's and parent's names to sing goodbye—sway a goodbye hand to the triple meter

(There are only 9 activities above; 12-14 are to be planned by repeating categories.)

Infants Music Lesson Plan 5

Choose 3-4 Duple and Triple Rhythms and insert into the Lesson Plan where appropriate.
Choose 3-4 Major and Minor Tonal Patterns and insert into the Lesson Plan where appropriate.

CATEGORY	MATERIALS	DOVETAILING OF MODE / METER / SPECIALTY	ACTIVITY
Hello Song	"Hello Song" Music Together—Sticks Song Collection, p. 13	Major Duple Singing & Pat / Clap the Duple Meter	Sit in a circle and sway back and forth gently on the macrobeats—sing close to each baby so (s)he can focus on your mouth
Bouncing Song / Lap Song			
Finger Play / Body Awareness			
Peek-a-Boo Song			
Steady Beat Activity with Instruments			
Dancing Song			
Rocking Song			
Large Gross Motor Activity with Traveling Movement			
Goodbye Song	"Goodbye, So Long, Farewell" by Ken Guilmartin Music Together—Sticks, p. 45	Major Triple Swaying & Pat / Clap / Clap the Triple Meter	Back to sitting in a circle—use each of the infant's and parent's names to sing goodbye—sway a goodbye hand to the triple meter

(There are only 9 activities above; 12-14 are to be planned by repeating categories.)

Infants Music Lesson Plan 6

Choose 3-4 Duple and Triple Rhythms and insert into the Lesson Plan where appropriate.
Choose 3-4 Major and Minor Tonal Patterns and insert into the Lesson Plan where appropriate.

CATEGORY	MATERIALS	DOVETAILING OF MODE / METER / SPECIALTY	ACTIVITY
Hello Song	"Hello Song" Music Together—Sticks Song Collection, p. 13	Major Duple Singing & Pat / Clap the Duple Meter	Sit in a circle and sway back and forth gently on the macrobeats—sing close to each baby so (s)he can focus on your mouth
Bouncing Song / Lap Song			
Finger Play / Body Awareness			
Peek-a-Boo Song			
Steady Beat Activity with Instruments			
Dancing Song			
Rocking Song			
Large Gross Motor Activity with Traveling Movement			
Goodbye Song	"Goodbye, So Long, Farewell" by Ken Guilmartin Music Together—Sticks, p. 45	Major Triple Swaying & Pat / Clap / Clap the Triple Meter	Back to sitting in a circle—use each of the infant's and parent's names to sing goodbye—sway a goodbye hand to the triple meter

(There are only 9 activities above; 12-14 are to be planned by repeating categories.)

Infants Music Lesson Plan 7

Choose 3-4 Duple and Triple Rhythms and insert into the Lesson Plan where appropriate.
Choose 3-4 Major and Minor Tonal Patterns and insert into the Lesson Plan where appropriate.

CATEGORY	MATERIALS	DOVETAILING OF MODE / METER / SPECIALTY	ACTIVITY
Hello Song	"Hello Song" Music Together—Sticks Song Collection, p. 13	Major Duple Singing & Pat / Clap the Duple Meter	Sit in a circle and sway back and forth gently on the macrobeats—sing close to each baby so (s)he can focus on your mouth
Bouncing Song / Lap Song			
Finger Play / Body Awareness			
Peek-a-Boo Song			
Steady Beat Activity with Instruments			
Dancing Song			
Rocking Song			
Large Gross Motor Activity with Traveling Movement			
Goodbye Song	"Goodbye, So Long, Farewell" by Ken Guilmartin Music Together—Sticks, p. 45	Major Triple Swaying & Pat / Clap / Clap the Triple Meter	Back to sitting in a circle—use each of the infant's and parent's names to sing goodbye—sway a goodbye hand to the triple meter

(There are only 9 activities above; 12-14 are to be planned by repeating categories.)

Infants Songs Collection
Indexed by Music Activity
Birth thru 1

NOTE: The follow songs are organized by suggested activity categories. The music for them may be found in well-known publications or on the Internet.

Bouncing Songs / Lap Songs. Each lesson should contain songs where the infant is bounced in the parent's lap to the steady beat of the music. Different positions can be used when participating in bouncing activities where the infant can face outwards towards the other infants in the circle or the infant faces the parent. Some songs may include surprises, such as where the infant is lifted from under the arms into the air or supporting under their legs and bottoms to lift them up while you roll back as to "whoa" the horses. This always produces giggles and smiles. In this activity the infant feels and hears that steady beat internally and externally while enjoying the bonding and closeness of being in their parent's lap and having the parent's undivided attention. Movement stimulates and charges the brain as infants learn through play; moving and being moved in the environment around them.

- A Ride To Bed .... Triple / Major
- Allee Galloo (Music Together-Triangle) CD#21-bounce and swing back with them in lap on whee .... Triple / Major
- Ally Bally (Music Together-Triangle) CD#19 .... Duple / Major
- Bim Bam (Music Together-Maracas) rock & tap steady beat .... Duple / Minor
- Dance To Your Daddy (Music Together-Flutes) .... Triple / Minor
- Dance With Me (Music Together-Triangle) CD#3 .... Duple & Triple / Major
- Donkey Riding bouncing .... Duple / Major
- Horsey, Horsey (www.youtube.com/watch?v=kfPKWCITnps) .... Triple / Major
- I'm a Little Horsey (Bouncing Song) (Music Copy) .... Duple / Major
- Jack Be Nimble (Music Together-Maracas) .... Triple Rhythmic Chant
- Li'L 'Liza Jane (Music Together-Bongs) CD#21 .... Duple / Major / Partner Songs
- Pop Goes The Weasel (pop up the baby on "pop") .... Triple / Major
- Ride-O bouncing .... Duple / Major
- Ride a Little Horsey bouncing .... Duple Rhythmic Chant
- Riding In A Buggy .... Duple / Major
- See How I'm Jumping (Music Together-Bongos) Sing Bouncing & Rocking .... Duple / Minor

She'll Be Comin' Round The Mountain (Music Together-Bongos) .... Duple / Major

Sweet Potato (Music Together-Babies) (www.youtube.com/watch?v=0cr1dczj-yM) .... Duple / Major

There's a Little Wheel-a-Turning (Music Together-Babies) .... Duple / Major

This Is The Way The Ladies Ride .... Triple / Major

To Market (Music Together-Babies) .... Triple Rhythmic Chant

Trot Old Joe (Music Together-Bells) .... Duple / Major

Trot to Grandma's House (Music Together-Babies) .... Duple / Major

Trot, Trot, Trot (Bouncing song) (music copy) .... Duple / Major

What'll I Do With The Baby-O (www.songsforteaching.com/folk/index.htm) .... Duple / Major

William Tell's Ride (Music Together-Babies) bounce (www.youtube.com/watch?v=xoHECVnQC7A) .... Duple / Major & Minor

Finger Play / Body Awareness. Finger play activities allow for fine motor exercises and language development growth opportunities. These songs/poems are more stationary and can lead into songs having to do with the same subject matter, such as rocking songs or lullabies with resonator bars. Parents should mirror the teacher as the song is sung, as parents show infants where their "body parts" are so they can tap them, etc.

Bees .... Duple / Major

Bingo .... Duple / Major

Brother John .... Duple / Major / Round

Clap Your Hands (Music Together-Drums) tap body parts then add instruments .... Duple / Mixolydian on D

Clap Your Hands .... Duple / Major

Cock-A-Doodle-Doo! .... Duple / Major

Deedle Dumpling Song (Music Together-Bells) .... Duple / Dorian

Diddle Diddle Dumpling (use with hands and feet) .... Duple Rhythmic Chant

Doctor Foster .... Triple / Major

Eensy, Weensey Spider (Music Together-Bongos) CD#15 .... Triple (or Compound Duple) / Major

Five Little Mice (Music Together-Maracas) then use instruments to be mice scampering away .... Duple Rhythmic Chant

Five Little Monkeys .... Duple / Major

Girls and Boys Come Out to Play .... Triple / Major

Head, Shoulders, Knees, and Toes .... Duple or Triple Rhythmic Chant, or if sung Duple / Major

Here Is a Bunny (Music Together-Triangle) CD#31—first use fingers then get hoops, be a hopping bunny .... Triple Rhythmic Chant

Here Is the Beehive (Music Together-Fiddle) .... Triple Rhythmic Chant

Hickory Dickory Dock .... Duple Rhythmic Chant

Hot Cross Buns (use later on drums) .... Duple / Major

I've Got The Rhythm In My Head (Music Together-Fiddle) .... Duple / Major

Jack Be Nimble .... Triple / Major

Little Bo Peep .... Duple / Major

London Bridge .... Duple / Major

Mary, Mary, Quite Contrary .... Duple / Major

Old McDonald .... Duple / Major

One Potato .... Triple / Major

Open and Shut Them (Music Together-Bongos) CD#4 .... Duple / Major

Pat a Cake (use later with sticks) .... Triple / Major

Pease Porridge Hot .... Duple / Major

Polly, Put the Kettle On .... Triple / Major

Pussy-Cat, Pussy-Cat .... Triple / Major

Ride a Cock Horse to Banbury Cross .... Triple / Major

Round and Round the Garden .... Triple Rhythmic Chant

Round and Round the Haystack (scarf-peek-a-boo/finger play)
.... Triple Rhythmic Chant

Russian Folk Song (Music Together-Maracas) also known as "May There Always Be Sunshine" rocking song .... Duple / Major

Sally Go Round the Sun .... Triple / Major

Seesaw Margery Daw .... Triple / Major

Sing a Song of Sixpence .... Duple / Major

Slowly, Slowly .... Duple Rhythmic Chant

Sneak and Peek (Music Together-Drum) scarves .... Duple / Dorian on D

Star Light, Star Bright .... Mixed Meter / Major

Ten Fingers (Music Together-Triangle) .... Duple Rhythmic Chant

The Grand Old Duke of York .... Duple / Major

The Muffin Man .... Duple / Major

The Snail and The Mouse (Music Together-Drum) ....Duple Rhythmic Chant

The Wheels on the Bus .... Duple / Major

There's A Cobbler (Music Together-Drum) sticks ....Duple Rhythmic Chant

This Little Cow Eats Grass .... Triple / Major

This Little Light of Mine (Music Together-Fiddle)................................. Duple / Major

This Old Man (Music Together-Bongos) CD#8....................................... Duple / Major

Three Blind Mice (steady beat) drums .... Triple / Major

Three Little Kittens ....Triple / Major

To Market, To Market..Triple / Major

Two Little Blackbirds (Music Together-Triangle) CD#26......................... Duple / Major

Two Little Eyes ....Duple Rhythmic Chant

Peek-a-Boo Songs. This category is songs where parent and child can play peek-a-boo with scarves. Use each infant's name in the song while looking straight at that infant. This creates bonding between parent and child as parent proceeds to cover infant and finds him/her. The parent can also cover up so the infant can pull off the scarf and find the parent. This develops a sense of trust, an element of surprise and excitement, which infants begin to anticipate. Later, when infants are comfortably mobile, they can help find each of the other infants as they are covered up. This builds a sense of friendship and community. These scarves can also be used as parent / infant dance movements in dance activities.

Allee Galloo (Music Together-Triangle) CD#21—use scarves to beat & throw/catch/play hide & seek)..Triple / Major

Dance With Me (Music Together-Triangle) CD#3—use scarves for Peek-a-boo version) .... Duple & Triple / Major

I See You My Darling Scarves/peek-a-boo ....Duple / Major

I'm Hiding (Music Together-Triangle) rap with scarves ....Duple Rhythmic Chant

Knockin' At My Window scarves or drums .... Duple / Major

Little Johnny Brown (Music Together-Bongos) CD#19—scarves)
.... Duple / Natural Minor

Round and Round the Haystack (scarves/finger play) ....Triple Rhythmic Chant

Sneak and Peek (Music Together-Drums) scarves........................ Duple / Dorian on D

Who's That? (Music Together-Babies and Bells) scarves .... Duple / Major

Steady Beat Activities Utilizing Instruments. (sticks, drums, shakers, resonator bars, jingles, scarves). Have at least three songs utilizing each of the instruments listed so the infants can hear as well as feel the steady beats and use instruments to match the beats. Infants will need to be manipulated at first, and then later will grow into tapping the drums by themselves or tapping sticks together. The teacher is always modeling to the parent in this class so the parent can manipulate the infant. Nursery rhymes are great for this, and teacher and parents alike should sing or say the nursery songs or rhymes using exaggerated vocal inflection to hold the infant's attention.

A Ram Sam Sam (Music Together-Fiddle) .... Duple / Major

Apples and Cherries (Music Together-Fiddle) .... Duple / Major / Tonal Round

Baa, Baa Little Star (Music Together-Triangle) CD#20—sticks
....Duple / Major / Instrumental Play Along

Biddy Biddy (Music Together-Drums) shakers or jingles .... Duple / Major

Bim Bam (Music Together-Maracas) .... Duple / Minor

Bongo Jam (Music Together-Bongos) CD#14—Instrumental   instrument jam
....Duple / Major / Instrumental Play Along

Breezes (Music Together-Triangle) CD#12—dance free style with scarves
....Triple / Mixolydian on D

Canoe Song (Music Together-Bongos) CD#20—drums or sticks .... Duple / Minor

Chatter With The Angels shakers .... Duple / Major

Clap Your Hands (Music Together-Drums) ....Duple / Mixolydian on D

Drummers Marching (Music Together-Triangle) CD#23 .... Triple / Minor

Frere Jacques (Music Together-Maracas)
 ....Duple / Major / Vocal & Instrumental Ostinatos

Hop Ol' Squirrel (Music Together-Maracas) drum .... Duple / Major

Hot Cross Buns (use on drums) .... Duple / Major

I'm A Bell (Music Together-Maracas) .... Triple / Minor

I'm Hiding (Music Together-Triangle) rap with scarves ....Duple Rhythmic Chant

I've Got The Rhythm In My Head (Music Together-Fiddle) .... Duple / Major

Knockin' At My Window Drums or Scarves .... Duple / Major

Land of the Silver Birch drums.. Duple / Minor

Little Johnny Brown (Music Together-Bongos) CD#19—scarves
.... Duple / Natural Minor

Mr. Frog Went A Courtin' (steady beat with sticks or shakers).............. Duple / Major

Muffin Man (shakers to the steady beat)... Duple / Major

Nothin' Blues (Music Together-Triangles) CD#2—steady beat with shakers or other percussion .... Duple / Major in Blues Style

Pat-a-Cake Pat-a-Cake (use with sticks) .... Triple / Major

Peas Porridge Hot (Music Together-Maracas)..........................Duple Rhythmic Chant

Rain Song (Music Together-Triangle) CD#9—sticks or drums
.... Duple / Dorian on D

She'll Be Comin' Round The Mountain (Music Together-Bongos) use instruments for special effects .... Duple / Major

Slowly, Slowly (drums) .... Duple Rhythmic Chant

Ten Fingers (Music Together-Triangle) use jingles .... Duple Rhythmic Chant

The Snail and The Mouse (Music Together-Drums) .... Duple Rhythmic Chant

There's A Cobbler (Music Together-Drums) sticks .... Duple Rhythmic Chant

This Old Man (Music Together-Bongos) CD#8—different percussion instruments
.... Duple / Major

This Train (Music Together-Drums) shakers
.... Duple / Dorian on D (Countermelodies)

Three Blind Mice (steady beat) drums or shakers .... Triple / Major

Train Is a-Comin' (Music Together-Bongos) CD#12—shakers .... Duple / Major

Train To the City (Music Together-Maracas) shakers .... Duple / Major

Twinkle Twinkle Little Star (resonator bars in the tonic chord or jingle sticks)
.... Duple / Major

Walking Through the Woods (Music Together-Bongos) CD#6—scarves
.... Triple / Minor

When Johnny Comes Marching Home Again Sticks or Shakers (http://bussongs.com/songs/when-johnny-comes-marching-home-again.php)
.... Triple / Minor

Who's That? (Music Together-Bells) Drum .... Duple / Major

Rhythm and Tonal Patterns. Short and simple 2-4 beat rhythmic examples, both duple and triple meter patterns (quarter and eighth note rhythms) and 3-note easy solfége patterns (So-Mi-Do for major, Mi-Do-La for minor) are presented by the teacher and echoed by parents so infants can be bathed in rhythmic and tonal patterns taken both from their music and simply created. The teacher chants the neutral syllable "ba" for rhythm patterns, and sings the neutral syllable "bum" for tonal patterns. These patterns can be taken from the rhythm and tonal flash cards in Book 1A of the Knauss Music Curriculum. These patterns can also be taken from the songs just sung, or in the next song to be sung, to help establish tonality (major or minor) or rhythmic meter (duple or triple). These short patterns become the building blocks for children to later identify in music heard or sung, or even to create music of their own. Just like language is learned from words to phrases to sentences, so music is learned the same way; rhythmic and tonal patterns to phrases to creative songs. These patterns help develop a musical vocabulary, which also helps develop memory skills, an important focus skill for K-12 grades and beyond.

Simple rhythm patterns of quarter and eighth notes on neutral syllable "ba"
Complex rhythm patterns of any combinations on neutral syllable "ba"
Duple and Triple rhythm patterns from Book 1A of Knauss Music Curriculum
Simple tonal patterns of Do-Mi-So using neutral syllable "ba"
Simple tonal patterns of La-Do-Mi using neutral syllable "ba"
Tonal patterns from Book 1A of Knauss Music Curriculum

Group Dance Activities. Dance activity songs can help develop large gross motor skills, as well as coordination and spatial awareness. Circle dance activities encourage a sense of community and cooperation where everyone moves together. Non-mobile infants are carried at first, but as they become mobile, they can join in the movement in whatever ways comfortable. These songs can be sung songs or recordings of classical music. The teacher should choose selections that allow for a circle dance where infants can circle right and left and then be spun around, or movement in towards the middle of the circle and back out. The best songs are ones that can be sung while danced, because of the combination of language and movement. These songs can be circle dances or children's games, such as London Bridge, or Ring Around the Rosie, or Did You Ever See A Lassie (where infants can swing this way and that).

Classical Instrumental Pieces—do simple circle dances with mom & baby (Circle left/right; move in center lift babies up together; swing side to side; spin around) .... see Movement Exploration publication and Keeping the Beat CD

Classical Music excerpts: Mozart's Divertimento; Handel's Water Music; etc. .... see Keeping the Beat CD

Dancing With Teddy (Music Together-Maracas) .... Triple / Major

Did You Ever See A Lassie (music copy) (rock this way and that or spin this way and that etc.) .... Triple / Major

Everybody Loves Saturday Night (Music Together-Drum) .... Duple / Major

Goin' To Boston (Music Together-Fiddle) .... Duple / Mixolydian on C

London Bridge .... Duple / Major

Mariá Isabel (Music Together-Triangles) CD#18 .... Duple / Major

Merry Go Round (Music Together-Babies) .... Triple / Minor

Mountain Dew (Music Together-Bongos) CD#16
.... Triple (or Compound Duple) / Major

Palo, Palo (Music Together-Bongos) CD#10—treat like conga line .... Duple / Major

Rig-a-Jig-Jig (Music Together-Drum) .... Triple / Major

Ring Around The Rosie .... Triple / Major

Shoo Fly (Music Together-Bongos) CD#17 .... Duple / Major

Simple Gifts (Music Together-Flute) .... Duple / Major / Instrumental Play Along

Skip To My Lou (Music Together-Triangles) CD#7 .... Duple / Major

Tingalayo (Music Together-Babies & Tambourine) .... Duple / Major

Rocking Songs. Rocking songs can be songs that are sung or recorded music that is played. Choose selections that establish a comfortable rocking beat for parent and infant. Rocking develops the inner ear which helps with spatial awareness, balance, and coordination, as well as allowing infants to learn how to calm themselves, all done in a wonderful activity that focuses on bonding parent and infant. This should be explained to parent (apart from the flow of the class) so they realize the importance of this activity. Rocking motions can be forward and backward or side to side. These motions can be changed with each different part of the music (if the music features different sections) and done by standing or sitting, as well as different positions facing infant out or in towards parent, or even by swinging position or flying position.

All Night, All Day .... Duple / Major

All The Pretty Horses (Music Together-Babies and Flute)
.... Duple / Minor (Aeolian or Natural)

Ally Bally (Music Together-Triangle) CD#19 .... Duple / Major

Arirang (Music Together-Drums) .... Triple / Do Pentatonic on G with accidental Bb

Baby's Boat .... Triple / Major

Bim Bam (Music Together-Maracas) .... Duple / Minor

Bye Baby Bunting .... Duple / Major

Dance With Me (Music Together-Triangle) CD#3 .... Duple & Triple / Major

Golden Slumbers (Beatles) .... Triple / Major

Greensleeves (Music Together-Bongos) CD#18 .... Triple / Harmonic Minor

Hush Little Baby .... Duple / Major

My Bonnie (Music Together-Bongos) CD#24 .... Triple / Major

Nothin' Blues (Music Together-Triangle) CD#2 .... Duple / Major in Blues Style

Oh How Lovely Is The Evening German folksong .... Triple / Major / Vocal Round

Scarborough Fair (Simon & Garfunkel) .... Triple / Minor

Shenandoah (Music Together-Fiddle) .... Duple / Major

Simple Gifts (Music Together-Babies and Flute)
.... Duple / Major / Instrumental Play Along

Sleep, Baby Sleep .... Duple / Major

Sleepyhead (Music Together-Bongos) CD#13 .... Duple / Major

The Riddle Song (Music Together-Flutes) .... Duple / Major

The Water Is Wide (Music Together-Triangle) CD#35 .... Duple / Major

Large Gross Motor Activity / Traveling Movement. Songs that are active and have infants up and moving, if they are mobile. They will improve a child's coordination, balance, and spatial awareness. These songs can be songs about different types of movement such as crawling, marching, twisting, etc. These songs can be sung first stationary or bouncing to the beat or using body percussion and then sung with traveling movement. Parents perform the movements while carrying the infant if infant is not yet mobile enough to perform the movement.

A Ram Sam Sam (Music Together-Fiddle) .... Duple / Major

All Around The Kitchen (Music Together-Maracas)
.... Duple / Three classic blues forms of 12-bar, 8-bar, & 16-bar on A Minor

Crawdad (Music Together-Fiddle) .... Duple / Major

Drummers Marching (Music Together-Triangle) CD#23 .... Triple / Minor

I'm A Rollin'/Walkin' movement... Duple / Major

Jumpin' Josie (Music Together-Maracas) .... Duple / Do Pentatonic on D

Ladybug (Music Together-Triangle) CD#17—movement improvisation
....Triple / Dorian Implied

See How I'm Jumping (Music Together-Bongos) CD#7 .... Duple / Minor

The Monkey Stomps stationary & travel movement............................. Duple / Major

Tingalayo (Music Together-Babies & Tambourine) movement or stick horses (www.youtube.com/watch?v=trCOfgwikjY)... Duple / Major

Train Is a-Comin' (Music Together-Bongos) CD#12—shakers .... Duple / Major

Walk All Around/Tap On Your Sticks (movement/sticks) .... Duple / Major

Walk Together Children travel movement
(www.youtube.com/watch?v=inZzny9ACzE) .... Duple / Major

Walk Walk Walk Walk (music copy) travel movement........................... Duple / Major

William Tell's Ride (Music Together-Babies and Maracas) bounce w/ stick horses (www.youtube.com/watch?v=xoHECVnQC7A)...................... Duple / Major and Minor

Hello / Goodbye Songs. Each lesson should contain a "Hello Song" and a "Good-bye Song." These songs may be two different ones, one for Hello and one for Goodbye, or they may be the Hello song with the lyrics changed for Goodbye. These remain the same for the entire class semester. During the hello and goodbye songs, each child's name is sung with a steady beat activity by using a body percussion activity. The Hello song signals the start of class, recognizes the specialness of each child as their name is sung, and allows for repetition (the same song) and variety as well (varying the beat activities). Also sing the names of any guests visiting for the class, such as friends or relatives (aunts, uncles, or grandparents).

Good Morning .... Triple / Major

Goodbye Now (tune of Good Morning) .... Triple / Major

Goodbye Song (tune of Twinkle, Twinkle Little Star) .... Duple / Major

Hello Song (from Music Together-Bongos) CD #1 .... Duple / Major

Hello Song (tune of Twinkle, Twinkle Little Star) .... Duple / Major

What Are You Wearing? .... Duple / Major

Familiar songs with which to change words to Hello or Goodbye:
Clap, Clap, Clap Your Hands
Go Tell Aunt Rhodie
Mary Had A Little Lamb
The More We Get Together
This is the Way We Wash Our Clothes

Infants Music Together Books Index

The Music Together Books included in this index are:

Music Together: Tambourine Song Collection
Music Together: Fiddle Song Collection
Music Together: Triangle Song Collection
Music Together: Drum Song Collection
Music Together: Bongos Song Collection
Music Together: Maracas Song Collection
Music Together: Bells Song Collection
Music Together: Sticks Song Collection
Music Together: Flute Song Collection
Music Together: Summer Songs 1
Music Together: Summer Songs 2
Music Together: Summer Songs 3
Music Together: Babies
Music Together: Family Favorites Songbook for Teachers

Music Together: Tambourine Song Collection

Guilmartin, K.K. & Levinowitz, L.M. (2004, 2007). *Music together: Tambourine song collection*. Princeton, NJ: Music Together LLC. www.musictogether.com. (CD, 2007). CD#: MTTA13-CD.

Contents

Betty Martin (Traditional)	p. 19	Duple / Major
Cradle Song (W. Blake & K. Guilmartin)	p. 29	Duple / Major
Ding Dong, Ding Dong (Traditional)	p. 41	Duple / Major / Tonal Round
Good News (Traditional African American Spiritual)	p. 45	Duple / Major
Goodbye, So Long, Farewell (K. Guilmartin)	p. 47	Triple / Major
Green and Blue (K. Guilmartin)	p. 22	Triple Rhythmic Chant
Hello Song (K. Guilmartin)	p. 13	Duple / Major
Hey Ya Na (Traditional Native American Apache)	p. 23	Duple / Natural Minor or Dorian
Hippity, Happity, Hoppity (Doug Morris)	p. 36	Triple Rhythmic Chant
Merry-Go Round (Lynn Lobban)	p. 39	Triple / Minor
Old Brass Wagon (Traditional)	p. 15	Duple / Major

One Little Owl (Traditional)	p. 21	Duple / Minor
Pawpaw Patch (Traditional)	p. 37	Duple / Major
Raisins and Almonds (Traditional)	p. 46	Triple / Minor
Ride-O (Traditional)	p. 16	Duple / Major
Round Robin (Rebecca Frezza)	p. 17	Duple / Major / Tonal Round
Scarborough Fair (Traditional)	p. 43	Triple / Minor
Secrets (K. Guilmartin, L. Levinowitz, & Linda Betlejeski)	p. 40	Duple Rhythmic Chant
See the Pony Galloping (Traditional)	p. 24	Triple / Major
Sneakin' 'Round the Room (K. Guilmartin)	p. 35	Duple / Minor (can be varied or Triple)
Tambourine Jam (K. Guilmartin)	p. 30	Duple / Major / Instrument Play Along with Minor contrasting section
This 'N' That (K. Guilmartin)	p. 42	Duple / Mixolydian (quasi-Cuban)
Tingalayo (Traditional Spanish)	p. 18	Duple / Major
Tricks With Sticks (K. Guilmartin)	p. 26	Duple Rhythmic Chant / Major Tonality in other sections
Wedding Dance (Traditional)	p. 25	Duple / Major with lowered 2nd, 6th, and 7th (Middle Eastern)

Music Together: Fiddle Song Collection

Guilmartin, K.K. & Levinowitz, L.M. (2006, 2009). *Music together: Fiddle song collection*. Princeton, NJ: Music Together LLC. www.musictogether.com. (CD, 2003). CD#: MTFI09-CD.

Contents

A Ram Sam Sam (Traditional)	p. 19	Duple / Major
Apples and Cherries (Traditional)	p. 17	Duple / Major / Tonal Round
Bela Boya (Traditional Bulgarian Folksong)	p. 25	Unusual Meter (7/8) / Implied Dorian Tonality
Butterfly (L. Levinowitz)	p. 40	Triple / Dorian on B
Can You Do This? (K. Guilmartin & L. Levinowitz)	p. 24	Duple / Lydian on C
Crawdad (Traditional)	p. 15	Duple / Major
Goin' To Boston (Traditional American Folksong)	p. 23	Duple / Mixolydian on C
Goodbye, So Long, Farewell (K. Guilmartin)	p. 46	Triple / Major

Hello Song (K. Guilmartin)	p. 13	Duple / Major
Here Is the Beehive (Traditional)	p. 33	Triple Rhythmic Chant
Hiné Ma Tov (Traditional Israeli Folksong)	p. 37	Duple / Dorian on E
I've Got The Rhythm In My Head (American Singing Game)	p. 36	Duple / Major
Lauren's Waltz (K. Guilmartin)	p. 29	Triple / Mixolydian on G (Middle section C Major / Instrumental Play Along)
Los Fandangos (Traditional Spanish Folksong)	p. 22	Triple / Minor
Marching and Drumming (American Civil War Melody)	p. 35	Triple / Natural Minor
Mississippi Cats (K. Guilmartin)	p. 41	Duple Rhythmic Chant
No More Pie (Traditional)	p. 39	Duple / Minor Blues
Old King Cole (K. Guilmartin)	p. 21	Duple / Natural Minor
Shady Grove (Traditional)	p. 28	Duple / Re Pentatonic based on C
Shenandoah (Traditional American Folksong)	p. 45	Duple / Major
Singin' Every Day (K. Guilmartin, South African Melody)	p. 43	Duple / Major
Sweet Potato (Traditional Afro-American Folksong)	p. 27	Duple / Major
The Sounds Of Fall (K. Guilmartin)	p. 16	Duple Rhythmic Chant
This Little Light Of Mine (Traditional)	p. 44	Duple / Major
Walking Song (K. Guilmartin)	p. 18	Duple / Mixolydian on D

Music Together: Triangle Song Collection

Guilmartin, K.K. & Levinowitz, L.M. (2003, 2006). *Music together: Triangle song collection*. Princeton, NJ: Music Together LLC. www.musictogether.com. (CD, 2006). CD#: MTTR12-CD.

Contents

Allee Galloo (Traditional)	p. 45	Triple / Major
Ally Bally (Traditional)	p. 29	Duple / Major
Baa, Baa, Little Star (K. Guilmartin)	p. 30	Duple / Major / Instrumental Play Along
Bird Song (Doug Morris)	p. 39	Triple / Phrygian on C
Breezes (K. Guilmartin)	p. 35	Triple / Mixolydian on D
Camels (K. Guilmartin)	p. 25	Duple / Implied Major with lowered 2nd
Can You Do What I Do? (Traditional)	p. 21	Duple Rhythmic Chant
Dance with Me (Traditional)	p. 14	Duple & Triple / Major
Drummers Marching (Linda Jessup)	p. 42	Triple / Minor

Goodbye, So Long, Farewell (K. Guilmartin)	p. 47	Triple / Major
Hello Song (K. Guilmartin)	p. 13	Duple / Major
Hey, Ho, Nobody Home (Traditional)	p. 28	Duple (Swing Rhythm) / Minor
I'm Hiding (K. Guilmartin)	p. 37	Duple Rhythmic Chant
Ladybug (Lynn Lobban)	p. 19	Triple / Dorian Implied
Mariá Isabel (Traditional Spanish Folksong)	p. 27	Duple / Major
Nothin' Blues (K. Guilmartin & J.C. Lewis)	p. 18	Duple / Major in Blues Style
Old Blue (Traditional)	p. 38	Duple / Mixolydian on D
Rain Song (K. Guilmartin)	p. 20	Duple / Dorian on D
Rolling a Round Ball (Sally Weaver)	p. 24	Triple / Dorian on C
Skip to My Lou (Traditional)	p. 41	Duple / Major
Stick Dance (K. Guilmartin)	p. 43	Unusual Meter (5/4) / Various Implied Tonalities (Lydian) and some Blues
Ten Fingers (Traditional)	p. 17	Duple Rhythmic Chant
The Train Song (Art Levinowitz)	p. 15	Duple / Major (Vocal Harmony Parts)
The Water is Wide (Traditional)	p. 46	Duple / Major
Two Little Blackbirds (K. Guilmartin)	p. 23	Duple / Major

Music Together: Drum Song Collection

Guilmartin, K.K. & Levinowitz, L.M. (2007, 2010). *Music together: Drum song collection*. Princeton, NJ: Music Together LLC. www.musictogether.com. (CD, 2012). CD#: MTDR13-CD.

Contents

Arirang (Traditional Korean Folksong)	p. 44	Triple / Do Pentatonic on G with accidental Bb)
Biddy Biddy (Traditional)	p. 14	Duple / Major
Clap Your Hands (Traditional)	p. 15	Duple / Mixolydian on D
Drum and Sing (K. Guilmartin)	p. 41	Duple / Minor
Duérmete Niño Bonito (Traditional Spanish Folksong)	p. 29	Triple / Minor
Everybody Loves Saturday Night (Traditional)	p. 45	Duple / Major
Goodbye, So Long, Farewell (K. Guilmartin)	p. 47	Triple / Major
Hello Song (K. Guilmartin)	p. 13	Duple / Major
John the Rabbit (Traditional)	p. 17	Duple / Major
Kookaburra (Traditional)	p. 43	Duple / Major
My Ball (L. Levinowitz)	p. 25	Unusual Meter (7/8) Rhythmic Chant

Play Along (K. Guilmartin) .... p. 30		Duple / Major / Instrumental Play Along
Playin' in the Kitchen (K. Guilmartin) .... p. 39		Duple Rhythmic Chant and Major Tonal Singing
Pussycat (J. Kuhns) .... p. 23		Mixed Triple / Phrygian on E
Rig-A-Jig-Jig (Traditional) .... p. 40		Triple / Major
Roll Over (Traditional) .... p. 21		Duple / Major
Sailing Song (L. Levinowitz) .... p. 26		Triple / Mixolydian on D
She Sells Sea Shells (K. Guilmartin) .... p. 19		Duple / Implied Dorian on D
Sneak and Peak (L. Levinowitz) .... p. 20		Duple / Dorian on D
The Snail and the Mouse (Traditional) .... p. 18		Duple Rhythmic Chant
There's a Cobbler (Traditional) .... p. 33		Duple Rhythmic Chant
They Come Back (K. Guilmartin) .... p. 35		Duple / Major
This Train (Traditional) .... p. 27		Duple / Dorian on D Countermelodies)
Ticking and Tocking (K. Guilmartin & L. Levinowitz) .... p. 24		Triple / Lydian on F
Tomorrow's Now Today (K. Guilmartin & L. Guilmartin) .... p. 46		Duple / Major

Music Together: Bongos Song Collection

Guilmartin, K.K. & Levinowitz, L.M. (2008). *Music together: Bongos song collection*. Princeton, NJ: Music Together LLC. www.musictogether.com. (CD, 2005). CD#: MTBO11-CD.

Contents

Bongo Jam (K. Guilmartin) .... p. 28		Duple / Major / Instrumental Play Along
Canoe Song (Traditional) .... p. 39		Duple / Minor
City Blues (K. Guilmartin) .... p. 45		Duple / Major
Ding-A-Ding (K. Guilmartin) .... p. 24		Duple / Dorian / Combinable
Down Under (K. Guilmartin) .... p. 43		Unusual Paired (6/8 & 4/4)
Eensy, Weensy Spider (Traditional American) .... p. 33		Triple (or Compound Duple) / Major
Every Day (K. Guilmartin) .... p. 15		Combined (Duple with Triplets) / Rhythm Activity
Fireworks (L. Levinowitz) .... p. 22		Triple / Rhythm Round
Goodbye, So Long, Farewell (K. Guilmartin) .... p. 47		Triple / Major
Greensleeves (Traditional English) .... p. 36		Triple / Harmonic Minor

Bitty Bops—Infants—Document 05

Hello Song (K. Guilmartin)	p. 13	Duple / Major
Hey, Diddle, Diddle (K. Guilmartin)	p. 17	Duple / Minor
Li'L 'Liza Jane / Funga Alafia (Traditional Afro-American)	p. 40	Duple / Major / Partner Songs
Little Johnny Brown (Traditional Afro-American)	p. 37	Duple / Natural Minor
Mountain Dew (Traditional Irish)	p. 34	Triple (or Compound Duple) / Major
My Bonnie (H. J. Fulmer)	p. 46	Triple / Major
Open and Shut Them (Traditional Flemish)	p. 16	Duple / Major
Palo, Palo (Traditional Dominican Republic)	p. 23	Duple / Major
See How I'm Jumping (Traditional Flemish)	p. 20	Duple / Minor
She'll Be Comin' 'Round the Mountain (Traditional American)	p. 14	Duple / Major
Shoo, Fly, Don't Bother Me (Frank Campbell & Billy Reeves)	p. 35	Duple / Major
Sleepyhead (Lyn Ransom)	p. 27	Duple / Major
This Old Man (Traditional)	p. 21	Duple / Major
Train is a-Comin' (Traditional Afro-American)	p. 25	Duple / Major
Walking Through the Woods (K. Guilmartin)	p. 19	Triple / Minor

Music Together: Maracas Song Collection

Guilmartin, K.K. & Levinowitz, L.M. (2005, 2008). *Music together: Maracas song collection*. Princeton, NJ: Music Together LLC. www.musictogether.com.

Contents

All Around The Kitchen (Traditional)	p. 18	Duple / Three classic blues forms of 12-bar, 8-bar, & 16-bar on A Minor
Bim Bam (Traditional)	p. 22	Duple / Minor
Brincan Y Bailan (Traditional)	p. 36	Duple / Minor
Cloud Song (Linda Jessup)	p. 41	Triple / Minor
Dancing With Teddy (K. Guilmartin)	p. 35	Triple / Major
Dee Da Dum (K. Guilmartin)	p. 37	Duple / Major / Jazz Style
Doodle (L. Levinowitz)	p. 27	Duple (Swing) / Dorian on D
Five Little Mice (Traditional)	p. 33	Duple Rhythmic Chant
Frère Jacques (Traditional)	p. 44	Duple / Major / Vocal and Instrumental Ostinatos
Goin' For Coffee (K. Guilmartin)	p. 30	Duple / Blues on C / Instrumental Play Along
Goodbye, So Long, Farwell (K. Guilmartin)	p. 46	Triple / Major
Hello Song (K. Guilmartin)	p. 13	Duple / Major

Hop Ol' Squirrel (Traditional)	p. 25	Duple / Major
I'm A Bell (L. Levinowitz)	p. 23	Triple / Minor
Jack Be Nimble (K. Guilmartin)	p. 40	Triple Rhythmic Chant
Jumpin' Josie (Traditional)	p. 14	Duple / Do Pentatonic on D
Pease Porridge Hot (Traditional)	p. 15	Duple Rhythmic Chant
Play the Drum (K. Guilmartin)	p. 43	Duple / Major
Russian Folk Song (Traditional)	p. 45	Duple / Major
Su La Li (Bonnie Light)	p. 29	Duple / Minor
The Sad Little Puppy (K. Guilmartin)	p. 39	Duple / Minor
Train To the City (Traditional)	p. 28	Duple / Major
Tsakonikos (Traditional)	p. 26	Unusual Meter (5/4) / Natural Minor
Wiggle! (L. Levinowitz)	p. 17	Duple / Major
William Tell's Ride (Rossini, arr. L. Ransom & K. Guilmartin)	p. 21	Duple / Major and Minor

Music Together: Bells Song Collection

Guilmartin, K.K. & Levinowitz, L.M. (2009). *Music together: Bells song collection*. Princeton, NJ: Music Together LLC. www.musictogether.com.

Contents

Brahms' Lullaby (Johannes Brahms)	p. 44	Triple / Major
By 'n' By (Traditional)	p. 29	Duple / Major
Celebration Song (Traditional Hasidic)	p. 23	Duple / Israeli Scale (Major with lowered 2nd)
De Colores (Traditional Mexican)	p. 27	Triple / Major
Deedle Dumpling (Chris Posluszny)	p. 25	Duple / Dorian
Foolin' Around (K. Guilmartin)	p. 30	Duple / Minor & Major / Instrumental
French Folk Song (Traditional French)	p. 37	Duple / Major
French Folk Song [Teacher Mixes] (on CD)		
Goodbye, So Long, Farewell (K. Guilmartin)	p. 45	Triple / Major
Hello Song (K. Guilmartin)	p. 13	Duple / Major
Hopping and Sliding (K. Guilmartin)	p. 18	Usual Paired (2/4 & 3/4) / Minor & Major
I'm Gonna Play Today (Traditional American)	p. 14	Duple / Major
Lukey's Boat (Traditional)	p. 26	Duple / Major
Me, You, and We (K. Guilmartin)	p. 36	Duple / Major
Misty Morning (K. Guilmartin)	p. 39	Triple / Minor (D Dorian & Natural)
Mr. Rabbit (Traditional)	p. 43	Duple / Major
My Lady Wind (K. Guilmartin)	p. 19	Duple / Major

Obwisana (Traditional Ghana)	p. 21	Duple / Major
Rhythms and Rhymes [Teacher Mixes] (on CD)		
Rhythms and Rhymes	p. 15	Duple Rhythm Chant
Robby Roly (K. Guilmartin)	p. 38	Duple / Minor
Robby Roly [Teacher Mixes] (on CD)		
Snowflakes (L. Levinowitz)	p. 22	Unusual (5/8) / Rhythmic Chant
Splishing and Splashing (K. Guilmartin)	p. 35	Duple with Triplets / Rhythmic Chant
The Bells of Westminster (Traditional)	p. 42	Duple / Major / Round & Countermelodies
The Bells of Westminster [Teacher Mixes] (on CD)		
Trot, Old Joe (Traditional)	p. 41	Duple / Major
Two Little Kitty Cats (Traditional)	p. 17	Duple / Minor
Who's That? (Traditional)	p. 33	Duple / Major

Music Together: Sticks Song Collection

Guilmartin, K.K. & Levinowitz, L.M. (2010). *Music together: Sticks song collection*. Princeton, NJ: Music Together LLC. www.musictogether.com. (CD, 2007). CD#: MTST11-CD.

Contents

Blow the Wind Southerly (Traditional)	p. 37	Triple / Major
Don Alfredo Baila (Traditional Catalonian)	p. 39	Duple / Major
Follow Me Down to Carlow (Traditional)	p. 17	Triple / Minor (or Dorian)
Goodbye, So Long, Farewell (K. Guilmartin)	p. 45	Triple / Major
Great Big Stars (Traditional Appalachian)		Duple / Major
Happy Puppy, Silly Cat (Sally Weaver)	p. 22	Unusual (7/8) / Major
Hello Song (K. Guilmartin)	p. 13	Duple / Major
Husha My Baby (Traditional South African)		Duple / Minor
I'm Freezing! (K. Guilmartin)	p. 24	Duple Chant
Jack-In-The-Box (Traditional)	p. 35	Triple / Rhythm Chant
Mary Wore a Red Dress (Traditional)	p. 18	Duple / Major
May All Children (K. Guilmartin)	p. 44	Multi-Metric (2/4, 3/4, 4/4) / Major
Mix It Up! (K. Guilmartin)	p. 38	Duple / G Mixolydian
Nigun (Traditional)	p. 25	Duple / Minor
Play Along, Too (K. Guilmartin)	p. 31	Duple / Major / Instrumental
Pop! Goes the Weasel (Traditional)	p. 28	Compound Triple (6/8) / Major
Ridin' in the Car (K. Guilmartin)	p. 15	Duple / Major

Roll That Little Ball (Traditional) .... p. 27   Duple / Major
Spin and Stop (L. Levinowitz) .... p. 19   Triple Minor
Stick Tune (K. Guilmartin) .... p. 21   Duple / D Mixolydian
The Love Song of Kangding (Traditional Sichuan Chinese)
....   Duple / Minor
The Tailor and the Mouse (Traditional) .... p. 36   Duple / Minor
Trot to Grandma's House (Traditional) .... p. 41   Duple / Major
Water Play (K. Guilmartin) ....   Triple Rhythm Activity
When the Saints Go Marching In (Traditional) .... p. 43   Duple / Major

Music Together: Flute Song Collection

Guilmartin, K.K. & Levinowitz, L.M. (2010). *Music together: Flute song collection*. Princeton, NJ: Music Together LLC. www.musictogether.com.

Contents

Aeolian Dance (K. Guilmartin)	p. 21	Duple / Aeolian / Sung Neutral Syllable & Danced
All the Pretty Little Horses (Traditional)	p. 45	Duple / Minor (Aeolian or Natural)
Dance to Your Daddy (Traditional)	p. 35	Triple / Minor
Dum Ditty Dum (Traditional)	p. 18	Duple / Major
Goodbye, So Long, Farewell (K. Guilmartin)	p. 46	Triple / Major
Harvest Dance (K. Guilmartin & L. Levinowitz)	p. 40	Triple / Major / Sung Neutral Syllable & Danced
Hello Song (K. Guilmartin)	p. 13	Duple / Major
Hey Lolly, Lolly (Traditional)	p. 14	Duple / Major
I Had a Little Frog (Traditional)	p. 15	Duple Rhythm Chant
I've Been Working on the Railroad (Traditional)	p. 43	Duple / Major
Jim Along Josie (Traditional)	p. 33	Duple / Major
Leaves Are Falling (Rebecca Frezza)	p. 27	Duple / Dorian on E / Round
Ran Tin Tinnah (Traditional Celtic)	p. 25	Duple / Major
Rocketship (Rebecca Frezza)	p. 36	Unusual (5/4) / Rhythmic Chant
Sandpiper (K. Guilmartin)	p. 20	Duple / Major
Saying and Doing (K. Guilmartin)	p. 23	Triple Rhythmic Chant
Shake Those 'Simmons Down (Traditional)	p. 28	Duple / Major
Simple Gifts (Traditional)	p. 30	Duple / Major / Instrumental Play Along
The Crow Song (Traditional)	p. 37	Duple / Major / Sung Neutral Syllable
The Earth is Our Mother (Traditional)	p. 19	Duple / Minor
The Riddle Song (Traditional)	p. 29	Duple / Major
The Three Ravens (Traditional)	p. 17	Duple / Minor
There's a Little Wheel a-Turnin' (Traditional)	p. 24	Duple / Major
Tum Balalaika (Traditional)	p. 41	Triple / Minor
Vengan a Ver (Traditional Argentinian)	p. 39	Duple / Major

Music Together: Summer Songs 1

Guilmartin, K.K. & Levinowitz, L.M. (2001). *Music together: Summer songs 1*. Princeton, NJ: Music Together LLC. www.musictogether.com.

Contents

A Ram Sam Sam (Traditional)	p. 20	Duple / Major
Deedle Dumpling (Chris Posluszny)	p. 33	Duple / Dorian
Goodbye, So Long, Farewell (K. Guilmartin)	p. 39	Triple / Major
Happy Puppy, Silly Cat (Sally Weaver)	p. 27	Unusual (7/8) / Major
Hello Song (K. Guilmartin)	p. 11	Duple / Major
Here Is the Beehive (Traditional)	p. 13	Triple Rhythmic Chant
Hey, Diddle, Diddle (K. Guilmartin)	p. 12	Duple / Minor
Hiné Ma Tov (Traditional Israeli Folksong)	p. 16	Duple / Dorian on E
I've Got The Rhythm In My Head (American Singing Game)	p. 17	Duple / Major
Jim Along Josie (Traditional)	p. 35	Duple / Major
Mariá Isabel (Traditional Spanish Folksong)	p. 37	Duple / Major
My Bonnie (H. J. Fulmer)	p. 38	Triple / Major
My Lady Wind (K. Guilmartin)	p. 21	Duple / Major
Play Along (K. Guilmartin)	p. 25	Duple / Major / Instrumental Play Along
Play the Drum (K. Guilmartin)	p. 15	Duple / Major
Rolling a Round Ball (Sally Weaver)	p. 30	Triple / Dorian on C
Ten Fingers (Traditional)	p. 19	Duple Rhythmic Chant
The Two Birds (Mother Goose)	p. 31	Duple Rhythm Chant with Triplets
Tomorrow's Now Today (K. Guilmartin & L. Guilmartin)	p. 24	Duple / Major
Tricks With Sticks (K. Guilmartin)	p. 22	Duple Rhythmic Chant / Major Tonality in other sections
Two Little Kitty Cats (Traditional)	p. 29	Duple / Minor

Music Together: Summer Songs 2

Guilmartin, K.K. & Levinowitz, L.M. (2007). *Music together: Summer songs 2*. Princeton, NJ: Music Together LLC. www.musictogether.com.

Contents

Allee Galloo (Traditional)	p. 37	Triple / Major
Butterfly (L. Levinowitz)	p. 36	Triple / Dorian on B
Crawdad (Traditional)	p. 15	Duple / Major
Doodle (L. Levinowitz)	p. 33	Duple (Swing) / Dorian on D
Eensy, Weensy Spider (Traditional American)	p. 18	Triple (or Compound Duple) / Major
Fireworks (L. Levinowitz)	p. 19	Triple Rhythmic Chant
Five Little Mice (Traditional)	p. 16	Duple Rhythmic Chant
Foolin' Around (K. Guilmartin)	p. 28	Duple / Minor & Major / Instrumental
Goodbye, So Long, Farewell (K. Guilmartin)	p. 40	Triple / Major
Hello Song (K. Guilmartin)	p. 13	Duple / Major
Here Is the Beehive (Traditional)	p. 31	Triple Rhythmic Chant
John the Rabbit (Traditional)	p. 25	Duple / Major
Mariá Isabel (Traditional Spanish Folksong)	p. 35	Duple / Major
Ridin' in the Car (K. Guilmartin)	p. 22	Duple / Major
She Sells Sea Shells (K. Guilmartin)	p. 23	Duple / Implied Dorian on D
Sleepyhead (Lyn Ransom)	p. 39	Duple / Major
Stick Dance (K. Guilmartin)	p. 26	Unusual Meter (5/4) / Various Implied Tonalities (Lydian) and some Blues
Su La Li (Bonnie Light)	p. 27	Duple / Minor
The Sad Little Puppy (K. Guilmartin)	p. 21	Duple / Minor
The Train Song (Art Levinowitz)	p. 17	Duple / Major (Vocal Harmony Parts)
Trot, Old Joe (Traditional)	p. 32	Duple / Major

Music Together: Summer Songs 3

Guilmartin, K.K. & Levinowitz, L.M. (2002). *Music together: Summer songs 3*. Princeton, NJ: Music Together LLC. www.musictogether.com.

Contents

Song	Page	Description
All the Pretty Little Horses (Traditional)	p. 27	Duple / Minor (Aeolian or Natural)
Apples and Cherries (Traditional)	p. 23	Duple / Major / Tonal Round
Baa, Baa, Little Star (K. Guilmartin)	p. 28	Duple / Major / Instrumental Play Along
Goodbye, So Long, Farewell (K. Guilmartin)	p. 42	Triple / Major
Hello Song (K. Guilmartin)	p. 13	Duple / Major
Here is a Bunny (Traditional)	p. 33	Triple Rhythm Chant
Hey, Ho, Nobody Home (Traditional)	p. 26	Duple (Swing Rhythm) / Minor
I Had a Little Frog (Traditional)	p. 14	Duple Rhythm Chant
Marching and Drumming (American Civil War Melody)	p. 18	Triple / Natural Minor
Me, You, and We (K. Guilmartin)	p. 15	Duple / Major
My Ball (L. Levinowitz)	p. 25	Unusual Meter (7/8) Rhythmic Chant
Obwisana (Traditional Ghana)	p. 17	Duple / Major
Old King Cole (K. Guilmartin)	p. 35	Duple / Natural Minor
Pussycat (J. Kuhns)	p. 21	Mixed Triple / Phrygian on E
Russian Folk Song (Traditional)	p. 41	Duple / Major
Sailing Song (L. Levinowitz)	p. 19	Triple / Mixolydian on D
See the Pony Galloping (Traditional)	p. 22	Triple / Major
Shake Those 'Simmons Down (Traditional)	p. 40	Duple / Major
Singin' Every Day (K. Guilmartin, South African Melody)	p. 39	Duple / Major
There's a Little Wheel a-Turnin' (Traditional)	p. 36	Duple / Major
Tingalayo (Traditional Spanish)	p. 37	Duple / Major

Music Together: Babies

Guilmartin, K.K. & Levinowitz, L.M. (2002). *Music together: Babies*. Princeton, NJ: Music Together LLC. www.musictogether.com.

Contents

Song	Page	Description
All the Pretty Little Horses (Traditional)	p. 33	Duple / Minor (Aeolian or Natural)
Allee Galloo (Traditional)	p. 39	Triple / Major
Bela Boya (Traditional Bulgarian Folksong)	p. 30	Unusual Meter (7/8) / Implied Dorian Tonality
Breezes (K. Guilmartin)	p. 27	Triple / Mixolydian on D
Dee Da Dum (K. Guilmartin)	p. 23	Duple / Major / Jazz Style
Eensy, Weensy Spider (Traditional American)	p. 25	Triple (or Compound Duple) / Major
Every Day (K. Guilmartin)	p. 22	Combined (Duple with Triplets) / Rhythm Activity
Fireworks (L. Levinowitz)	p. 26	Triple Rhythmic Chant
Goodbye, So Long, Farewell (K. Guilmartin)	p. 52	Triple / Major
Hello Song (K. Guilmartin)	p. 19	Duple / Major
Here Is the Beehive (Traditional)	p. 41	Triple Rhythmic Chant
Hey Ya Na (Traditional Native American—Apache)	p. 45	Duple / Natural Minor
Mary Wore a Red Dress (Traditional)	p. 50	Duple / Major
Merry-Go Round (Lynn Lobban)	p. 40	Triple / Minor
My Bonnie (H. J. Fulmer)	p. 51	Triple / Major
Obwisana (Traditional Ghana)	p. 43	Duple / Major
Simple Gifts (Traditional)	p. 34	Duple / Major / Instrumental Play Along
Sneakin' 'Round the Room (K. Guilmartin)	p. 49	Duple / Minor (can be varied for Triple)
Sweet Potato (Traditional Afro-American Folksong)	p. 29	Duple / Major
There's a Little Wheel a-Turnin' (Traditional)	p. 31	Duple / Major
Tingalayo (Traditional Spanish)	p. 32	Duple / Major
To Market (Traditional & K. Guilmartin)	p. 44	Triple Rhythm Chant
Trot to Grandma's House (Traditional)	p. 21	Duple / Major
Who's That? (Traditional)	p. 37	Duple / Major
William Tell's Ride (Rossini, arr. L. Ransom & K. Guilmartin)	p. 47	Duple / Major and Minor

Music Together: Family Favorites Songbook for Teachers

Guilmartin, K.K. & Levinowitz, L.M. (2009). *Music together: Family favorites songbook for teachers: Bringing harmony home*. Princeton, NJ: Music Together LLC. www.musictogether.com. ISBN: 978-0-615-32865-2.

Contents

Allee Galloo (Traditional)	p. 88	Triple / Major
Biddy Biddy (Traditional)	p. 26	Duple / Major
Dancing With Teddy (K. Guilmartin)	p. 84	Triple / Major
Goin' For Coffee (K. Guilmartin)	p. 70	Duple / Blues on C / Instrumental Play Along
Goodbye, So Long, Farewell (K. Guilmartin)	p. 96	Triple / Major
Hello Song (K. Guilmartin)	p. 22	Duple / Major
I've Been Working on the Railroad (Traditional)	p. 80	Duple / Major
John the Rabbit (Traditional)	p. 54	Duple / Major
May All Children (K. Guilmartin)	p. 92	Multi-Metric (2/4, 3/4, 4/4) / Major
Mississippi Cats (K. Guilmartin)	p. 62	Duple Rhythmic Chant
Obwisana (Traditional Ghana)	p. 76	Duple / Major
One Little Owl (Traditional)	p. 66	Duple / Minor
Palo, Palo (Traditional Dominican Republic)	p. 50	Duple / Major
Playin' in the Kitchen (K. Guilmartin)	p. 46	Duple Rhythmic Chant and Major Tonal Singing
Ridin' in the Car (K. Guilmartin)	p. 34	Duple / Major
She Sells Sea Shells (K. Guilmartin)	p. 42	Duple / Implied Dorian on D
Spin and Stop (L. Levinowitz)	p. 58	Triple Minor
Splishing and Splashing (K. Guilmartin)	p. 30	Duple with Triplets / Rhythmic Chant
Stick Tune (K. Guilmartin)	p. 38	Duple / D Mixolydian

Infants Music Play Index

Music Play: Book 1

Valerio, W., Reynolds, A., Bolton, B., Taggart, C., & Gordon, E. (2000). *Music play: Book 1: The early childhood music curriculum guide for parents, teachers and caregivers*. Chicago, IL: GIA Publications, Inc. Item #G-J236. ISBN: 1-57999-027-4.

The *Music Play* guide includes 57 songs and rhythm chants in a variety of tonalities and meters and over 200 music and movement activities designed to assist you in organizing sequential music and movement experiences for newborn and young children. Each of the songs and rhythm chants found in the guide is recorded on the accompanying compact disc or cassette.

Valerio, W., Reynolds, A., Bolton, B., Taggart, C., & Gordon, E. (1998). *Music play: CD: The early childhood music curriculum guide for parents, teachers and caregivers*. Chicago, IL: GIA Publications, Inc. Item #CD-426.

The beautiful full-color book and CD set includes photos of children engaged in music activities. The book includes notation and lesson plans adapted to the individual needs of each child, as well as a complete introduction to how young children learn when they learn music.

Contents

Songs Without Words (sing with tonal neutral syllable "bum") .... pp. 49-76

"Ring the Bells" .... p. 50 — Major / Duple
    Acculturation Tonal Pattern 1 — Major
    Imitation Tonal Pattern 1 — Major
    Imitation Tonal Pattern 2 — Major
    Assimilation Pattern Activities

"My Mommy is a Pilot" .... p. 52 — Major / Duple
    Acculturation Tonal Pattern 1 — Major
    Imitation Tonal Pattern 1 — Major
    Imitation Tonal Pattern 2 — Major
    Assimilation Pattern Activities

"Bumble Bee" .... p. 54 — Major / Multi-Metric (Unusual Paired 5/8 & Triple)
    Acculturation Tonal Pattern 1 — Major
    Imitation Tonal Pattern 1 — Major
    Imitation Tonal Pattern 2 — Major
    Assimilation Pattern Activities

"I Saw a Dinosaur" .... p. 56   Major / Duple
    (Acculturation, Imitation, Assimilation activities continue with each song)
"Winter Day" .... p. 58   Harmonic Minor / Unusual Paired (5/8)

"The Sled" .... p. 60   Harmonic Minor / Triple / ABA Form

"Pennsylvania Dreamin'" .... p. 62   Harmonic Minor / Triple
"Planting Flowers" .... p. 64   Melodic Minor / Triple
"Goldfish" .... p. 66   Dorian / Triple
"Dancing" .... p. 67   Dorian / Duple
"Jumping" .... p. 68   Dorian" / Triple
"Ocean Waves" .... p. 69   Dorian / Triple
"Country Dance" .... p. 70   Mixolydian / Triple
"Red Umbrella" .... p. 71   Dorian / Unusual Unpaired (7/8) / Ritardando

"Albany" .... p. 72   Mixolydian / Multi-Metric (Triple & Duple)

"Good-bye .... p. 73   Phrygian / Triple
"Stirring Soup" .... p. 74   Phrygian / Unusual Paired (5/8)

"Daydreams" .... p. 75   Locrian / Duple

Chants Without Words (chant with rhythm neutral syllable "ba") ....pp. 77-98

"Follow Me!" .... p. 78   Duple
"Stretch and Bounce" .... p. 80   Duple
"Walking With My Mom" .... p. 82   Duple / Accent
"Fireworks" .... p. 84   Duple / Crescendo / Subito
"Rolling" .... p. 86   Triple
"Popsicle" .... p. 88   Triple / Crescendo / Decrescendo / Same and Different

"Child Song" .... p. 90   Triple
"Snowflake" .... p. 92   Harmonic Minor (Recorded accompaniment) / Triple

"Rain" .... p. 94   Unusual Paired (5/8) / Timbre Awareness

"Panda" .... p. 95   Unusual Paired (5/8)
"Buggy Ride" .... p. 96   Unusual Unpaired (7/8) / Accent

"Wild Pony" .... p. 97   Unusual Unpaired (7/8) / Accent

"Train Ride" .... p. 98   Unusual Unpaired (7/8) / Accent

Songs With Words .... pp. 99-111

"Down By the Station"	p. 100	Major / Duple
"Jeremiah Blow the Fire"	p. 101	Major / Duple
"Roll the Ball Like This"	p. 102	Harmonic Minor / Triple
"My Pony Bill"	p. 103	Harmonic Minor / Triple
"Ni, Nah, Noh"	p. 104	Aeolian / Triple / Ritardando / Same and Different
"Bushes and Briars"	p. 105	Dorian / Triple / Same and Different
"To the Window"	p. 106	Dorian or Aeolian / Unusual Paired (5/8)
"Swinging"	p. 107	Mixolydian / Triple
"Jerry Hall"	p. 108	Mixolydian / Unusual Paired (5/8)
"The Wind"	p. 109	Lydian / Triple
"Poor Bengy"	p. 110	Phrygian / Duple
"North and South"	p. 111	Locrian / Duple

Chants With Words .... pp. 112-124

"My Mother, Your Mother"	p. 113	Duple
"Popcorn"	p. 114	Duple
"Go and Stop"	p. 115	Duple
"Sidewalk Talk"	p. 116	Duple
"This Little Piggy	p. 117	Triple
"Clackety Clack"	p. 118	Triple
"Hickety Pickety Bumble Bee"	p. 119	Triple
"Here is the Beehive"	p. 120	Triple / Tempo (Quick and Slow)
"Jump Over the Ocean"	p. 121	Triple
"Flop"	p. 122	Unusual Unpaired (7/8)
"In the Tub"	p. 123	Unusual Unpaired (7/8)
"Hop and Stop"	p. 124	Multi-Metric (Unusual Paired 5/8 & Triple)

Infants Nichol's Worth Books Index

A Nichol's Worth
Volumes 1, 2, 3, & 4

Nichol, Doug (1975). *A Nichol's worth. Volumes 1 & 2 (1975). Volumes 3 & 4 (1978).* Buffalo, NY: Tometic Associates LTD. Reprinted with permission. University Park, PA: The Pennsylvania State University Bookstore.

A collection of witty, folk-like songs in four volumes, featuring duple, triple, and multi-metric combined meters; in Major, Minor, Dorian, Mixolydian, Phrygian, Lydian, and multi-tonal modes; and in vocal textures of unison, combinable songs, partner songs, ostinatos, countermelodies, and rounds.

Contents

A Nichol's Worth, Volume I .... pp. 1-52

"Acceptance"	p. 42	Combined Meter (Duple with Triplets) / Minor / Unison
"Boy I'm Gonna Get Stuffed With Food"	p. 12	Triple / Dorian / Unison
"Changeable Chug-a-lug"	p. 50	Duple / Triple / Major / Combinable
"Do You Believe It?"	p. 26	Duple / Major / Partner
"Fireman, Fireman"	p. 5	Duple / Minor / Ostinato
"Freedom"	p. 32	Duple / Major / Countermelody
"Grandma Has a Habit"	p. 2	Triple / Mixolydian / Countermelody
"The Grasshopper and the Elephant"	p. 9	Duple / Phrygian / Unison
"Happiness is Giving"	p. 15	Duple / Mixolydian / Partner
"Hot Dog"	p. 4	Unusual Meter (5/8) / Major / Unison
"I Don't Believe It"	p. 27	Duple / Major / Partner
"I'm Your Friend"	p. 14	Duple / Mixolydian / Partner
"I Want to Be Lonely"	p. 22	Duple / Major / Unison
"I Would Give You the World"	p. 36	Triple / Major / Unison
"Let's Make It Christmas All the Time"	p. 16	Duple / Major / Countermelodies
"Look For the Bright Side"	p. 38	Duple / Major / Combinable
"Love Would Increase"	p. 44	Duple / Dorian / Countermelodies
"New Shoes"	p. 6	Duple / Major / Unison

"Nobody Cares" .... p. 40 — Duple / Lydian / Countermelodies
"One of These Days" .... p. 35 — Unusual (6/8 with Duple & Triple) / Mixolydian / Round
"Peas" .... p. 1 — Triple / Lydian / Unison
"The Secret" .... p. 30 — Duple / Minor / Unison
"The Squirrel" .... p. 8 — Triple / Phrygian / Unison
"There Won't Be Any to Save" .... p. 24 — Duple / Major / Unison
"Time" .... p. 46 — Duple / Major / Countermelody
"What Am I?" .... p. 28 — Duple / Mixolydian / Ostinato
"When I'm Thinking of You" .... p. 19 — Duple / Major / Combinable
"Where In the World Did I Put My Mittens?" ..... p. 10 — Duple / Major / Unison
"Who Says?" .... p. 20 — Duple / Mixolydian / Unison

A Nichol's Worth, Volume II .... pp. 1-52

"Autumn" .... p. 22 — Triple / Minor & Dorian / Countermelody
"Bangity Wangity Wapsy Boom" .... p. 1 — Triple / Major / Unison
"Boy, I Wish I Were Ninety Feet Tall" .... p. 2 — Triple / Dorian / Unison
"Come On You People" .... p. 51 — Duple / Major / Round
"Chug-a-lug Choo Choo" .... p. 29 — Unusual (5/8) / Major / Round
"The Eagle" .... p. 50 — Duple / Minor / Unison
"Eletelephony" .... p. 3 — Duple / Mixolydian / Unison
"Funny Shape" .... p. 20 — Triple / Lydian / Countermelodies
"Give a Little Love" .... p. 30 — Duple / Major / Combinable
"H-A-double P-I-N-E-double S" .... p. 8 — Duple / Major / Unison
"The Hootchy Kootchy Dance" .... p. 6 — Duple / Mixolydian / Countermelodies
"I Do Better When I Try My Best" .... p. 40 — Duple / Major / Countermelody
"I'm Tired of Bein' Busy" .... p. 42 — Duple / Major / Unison
"It's Not Too Bad to Be Me" .... p. 46 — Duple / Lydian / Combinable
"Living Spring" .... p. 10 — Combined (Duple with Triplets) / Major / Round
"Oh, It's Great to Be Living This Morning" ...... p. 34 — Duple / Major / Combinable
"The Old Swamp Band" .... p. 26 — Duple / Major / Unison
"Over" .... p. 39 — Duple / Major / Unison
"People Who Need Your Help" .... p. 16 — Duple / Major / Countermelodies
"Sam, Sam, the Butcher Man" .... p. 9 — Duple / Lydian / Ostinatos
"Snow" .... p. 44 — Triple / Major / Combinable

"Summer Is"	p. 11	Triple / Mixolydian / Round
"The Summer's Near"	p. 48	Duple / Minor / Unison
"Three Limericks"	p. 12	Triple / Mixolydian / Partner
"Turkey Struttin' 'Round"	p. 4	Duple / Mixolydian / Unison
"What Would the World Be Like Without Music?"	p. 14	Duple / Major / Combinable
"The Whistle"	p. 19	Duple / Major / Unison
"You Make Me Glad That I Know You"	p. 36	Duple / Major / Unison

A Nichol's Worth, Volume III ....pp. 1-31

"Be Thankful For Love"	p. 28	Duple / Major / Unison
"Cold Wind of Winter"	p. 8	Duple / Major / Unison
"Dancing Bear"	p. 13	Duple / Major / Unison
"Don't Be A Slob"	p. 9	Combined (Duple & Triple) / Lydian / Unison
"Do You Ever?"	p. 14	Triple / Major / Unison
"Elephants, Monkeys, and Leopards"	p. 5	Triple / Major / Combinable
"Farm, Farm, Farm, Farm"	p. 2	Duple / Major / Combinable
"The Grasswalker"	p. 22	Unusual (5/8) / Major / Combinable
"Gus"	p. 3	Triple / Dorian / Unison
"Had A Little Thought"	p. 20	Duple / Major / Partner
"I Love A Melody"	p. 21	Duple / Major / Partner
"It's All Pretend"	p. 10	Triple / Minor / Unison
"I Want To Be A Circus Clown"	p. 15	Triple / Mixolydian / Unison
"March"	p. 1	Duple / Major / Combinable
"The Middle of the Night"	p. 6	Duple / Phrygian / Unison
"Misery To A Kid"	p. 30	Duple / Major / Unison
"My Aminal"	p. 29	Duple / Minor / Unison
"My Secret Tree"	p. 24	Duple / Major / Unison
"Oh, I'll Build A Snowman"	p. 18	Triple / Minor / Partner
"Oh, Moe Is We"	p. 26	Duple / Major / Unison
"Old Folks"	p. 12	Duple / Major / Combinable
"Pancakes"	p. 25	Duple / Major / Unison
"Shiver"	p. 7	Duple / Major / Unison
"Song For Any Season"	p. 16	Duple / Mixolydian & Dorian / Countermelody
"Take A Look at Your Life"	p. 11	Unusual (7/8) / Major / Round
"We Share the World Together"	p. 4	Duple / Major / Combinable
"Why Don't They Feel Like Me"	p. 19	Triple / Minor / Partner

A Nichol's Worth, Volume IV .... pp. 1-39

"A Favorite Thing to Me"	p. 24	Duple / Major / Unison
"April Rain"	p. 16	Triple / Phrygian / Round
"Children Are Laughing"	p. 32	Duple / Major / Unison
"Come On and Laugh With Me"	p. 19	Duple / Major / Partner
"The Eefin' Song"	p. 28	Duple / Minor / Combinable
"February"	p. 1	Duple / Major / Unison
"I Can Feel the Beauty"	p. 17	Duple / Major / Unison
"I'd Like to Roller Skate on the Moon"	p. 38	Duple / Major / Unison
"I'm So Unhappy"	p. 18	Duple / Major / Partner
"It's Snowing"	p. 4	Triple / Major / Partner
"January"	p. 6	Duple / Major / Combinable
"Johnson Boys"	p. 30	Duple / Major / Countermelody
"Just Give Me a Cloudy Day"	p. 2	Duple / Major / Unison
"Let Me Be"	p. 27	Triple / Lydian / Countermelody
"Let's Play in the Snow"	p. 4	Triple / Major / Partner
"Magic Land"	p. 20	Duple / Major / Combinable
"Monkey Business"	p. 13	Duple / Mixolydian / Round
"My Little Friend"	p. 34	Duple / Major / Unison
"Oh, Yeah?"	p. 5	Triple / Dorian / Unison
"Rain"	p. 26	Triple / Major / Combinable
"Smile and Be Yourself"	p. 14	Duple / Major / Countermelody
"There Were Some Times"	p. 36	Duple / Major / Unison
"Things Are For Things"	p. 25	Unusual (Multi-Metric) / Major / Unison
"We Are Together"	p. 8	Duple / Major / Unison
"You'll Sound As Weird As Me"	p. 25	Triple / Multi-Tonal / Unison
"You Ought To"	p. 12	Triple / Minor / Unison
"You're As Good As All of the Rest"	p. 10	Triple / Dorian / Unison

Infants Movement with Instrumental Music

The Book of Movement Exploration: Can You Move Like This?

Feierabend, J., & Kahan, J. (2003). *The book of movement exploration: Can you move like this?* Chicago, IL: GIA Publications, Inc. ISBN 1-57999-264-1.

Feierabend, J. (2110). *First steps in classical music: Keeping the beat! (Compiled by John Feierabend)*. Chicago, IL: GIA Publications, Inc. CD#: CD-493

Book Contents

Theme 1: Awareness of Body Parts & Whole ....pp. 11-16

    1.1 Whole Body Movement.. p. 12
    1.2 Isolated Body Parts .... p. 13
    1.3 Leading with a Part .... p. 16
    1.4 Initiating with a Part .... p. 16

Theme 2: Awareness of Time ....pp. 17-18

    2.1 Quick and Slow Movement................................ p. 18
    2.2 Clock Time.. p. 18

Theme 3: Awareness of Space ....pp. 21-28

    3.1 Personal Space and General Space.................... p. 22
    3.2 Direct / Indirect Pathway (Straight / Twisted) .. p. 22
    3.3 Inward Movement (Narrow)............................... p. 24
    3.4 Outward Movement (Wide) .... p. 25
    3.5 Direction of Movement .... p. 27
    3.6 Distance of Movement .... p. 28

Theme 4: Awareness of Levels ....pp. 21-32

    4.1 High / Middle / Low .... p. 32

Theme 5: Awareness of Weight ....pp. 35-37

    5.1 Heavy / Light .... p. 36
    5.2 Strong / Gentle .... p. 37
    5.3 Tense / Relaxed... p. 37

Theme 6: Awareness of Locomotion .... **p. 49**

Theme 7: Awareness of Flow .... **pp. 43-46**

    7.1 Sudden / Sustained .... p. 44
    7.2 Sequential / Simultaneous .... p. 45
    7.3 Bound / Free .... p. 46

Theme 8: Awareness of Shape .... **pp. 49-50**

    8.1 Becoming Shapes .... p. 50

Theme 9: Awareness of Others .... **pp. 53-57**

    9.1 Partners .... p. 54
    9.2 Groups .... p. 57

Theme 10: Student Created Movement .... **pp. 59-63**

    10.1 Representative Movement .... p. 60
    10.2 Non-Representative Movement .... p. 63

CD Contents and Music Concepts

Excerpt time lengths range from 1:09 to 2:55:

1. Concerto No. 10 in C Major (Arcangelo Corelli).........Major / Duple / Tempo = MM132

2. Concerto No. 11 in Bb Flat Major: *Allemanda, Allegro* (Arcangelo Corelli)
....Major / Duple / Tempo = MM130

3. Concerto No. 12 in F Major (Arcangelo Corelli)
....Major / Duple Compound / Tempo = MM132

4. Concert in F Major: *Giga, Allegro* (Arcangelo Corelli)
....Major / Triple / Tempo = MM126

5. Gloria in D, RV 589: *Domini Fili* (Antonio Vivaldi)
....Major / Triple / Tempo = MM126

6. Suite and Dances: *Premier et deuxiéme contredanse* (Jean-Philip Rameau)
....Major / Duple / Tempo = MM130

7. Suite No. 3 in D, BWV 1068: *Gigue* (J .S. Bach)
....Major / Duple Compound / Tempo = MM120

8. Suite No. 4 in D, BWV 1069: *Gavotte* (J. S. Bach)
....Major / Duple / Tempo = MM136

9. Suite No. 4 in D, BWV 1069: *Rejouissance* (J. S. Bach)
....Major / Duple / Tempo = MM126

10. Suite No. 2 in b minor, BWV 1067: *Bourée I and II* (J. S. Bach)
.... Minor / Duple / Tempo = MM120

11. Suite No. 2 in b minor, BWV 1067: *Minuet* (J. S. Bach)
.... Minor / Triple / Tempo = MM132

12. Suite No. 2 in b minor, BWV 1067: Badinerie (J. S. Bach)
.... Minor / Duple / Tempo = MM126

13. Magnificat: Et exsultavit (J. S. Bach) .... Major / Triple / Tempo = MM122

14. Water Music: Allegro: (Gigue) (George Frideric Handel)
.... Major / Duple Compound / Tempo = MM136

15. Fireworks Music: Minuet II (George Frideric Handel)
.... Major / Triple / Tempo = MM132

16. Water Music: Minuet (George Frideric Handel) ...... Major / Triple / Tempo = MM124

17. Concerto grosso in D Major, Op. 1, No. 5: *Allegro* (Pietro Locatelli)
.... Major / Duple / Tempo = MM136

18. Concerto grosso in D Major, Op. 1, No. 9: *Allegro* (Pietro Locatelli)
.... Major / Triple / Tempo = MM136

19. Eine kliene Nachtmusik, K. 525: *Allegro* (Wolfgang Amadeus Mozart)
.... Major / Duple / Tempo = MM132

20. Eine kliene Nachtmusik, K. 525: *Rondo, Allegro* (Wolfgang Amadeus Mozart)
.... Major / Duple / Tempo = MM120

21. Symphony No. 40 in g minor, K. 550: *Allegro assai* (Wolfgang Amadeus Mozart)
.... Major / Duple / Tempo = MM126

22. Ballet Music from Faust: *Allegretto* (Charles Gounod)
.... Minor / Duple / Tempo = MM120

23. Gaîté Parisienne: Overture (Jacques Offenbach)..... Major / Duple / Tempo = MM126

24. Gaîté Parisienne: *Guadrille* and *Allegro* (Jacques Offenbach)
.... Major / Duple / Tempo = MM120

25. Gaîté Parisienne: *Allegro* and *Allegro* (Jacques Offenbach)
.... Major / Duple / Tempo = MM136

26. Hungarian Dances: No. 18 (Johannes Brahms)........ Minor / Duple / Tempo = MM136

27. Swan Lake: Spanish Dance (Peter Ilyich Tchaikovsky)
.... Major / Triple / Tempo = MM124

28. The Nutcracker: Overture (Peter Ilyich Tchaikovsky) ....Major / Duple / Tempo = MM128

29. Ancient Airs and Dances: Suite No. 1: Baletto detto "Il Conte Orlando" (Ottorino Respighi) ....Major / Duple / Tempo = MM126

30. Ancient Airs and Dances: Suite No. 2: Laura Soave (Ottorino Respighi) ....Major / Duple / Tempo = MM126

31. Háry János Suite: Viennese Musical Clock (Zoltan Kodaly) ....Major / Duple / Tempo = MM128

32. Pulcinella Suite: *Allegro* (Igor Stravinsky) ....Major / Duple / Tempo = MM126

33. Symphony No. 1 in D Major: Gavotte: *Non troppo allegro* (Sergei Prokofiev) ....Major / Duple / Tempo = MM120

34. Rodeo: Hoe-Down (Aaron Copeland) ....Major / Duple / Tempo = MM128

35. Romeo and Juliet: Preparation for the Ball (Dmitry Kabalevsky) ....Major / Duple / Tempo = MM126

36. The Comedians: Epilogue (Dmitry Kabalevsky) ....Major / Duple / Tempo = MM126

Notes for
BOOK 1: INFANTS

BITTY BOPS

BOOK 2: TODDLERS
PreK Music Curriculum
for
Ages 2 thru 3

How To Use *Bitty Bops—Toddlers* Music Curriculum

There are four main sections to *Bitty Bops—Toddler* Music Curriculum.

TODDLERS LESSON STRUCTURE & ACTIVITIES EXPLAINED
(1) *Bitty Bops—Toddlers* music teachers must first learn the Toddler Lesson Structure and explanation of Toddler Activities. **(See Document 11 and paragraphs in Document 14.)**

HOW TODDLERS LEARN MUSIC
(2) Dr. Edwin Gordon's research and publication explain how pre-K12 children learn, their responses, and how a teacher should interact with the student for each of the stages of:

    ACCULTURATION (Infants: Birth to Age 2-4)
    IMITATION (Toddlers: Ages 2-4 to 3-5)
    ASSIMILATION (Preschoolers: Ages 3-5 to 4-6)

All levels of *Bitty Bops* music teachers need to know what comprises these stages, how to recognize children's responses for each level, and how the *Bitty Bops* music teacher should interact rhythmically and tonally with the children on each level. For this level, *Bitty Bops—Toddlers* music teachers especially need to know the stages of IMITATION (Toddlers: Ages 2-4 to 3-5). **(See Document 12.)**

COMPILATION OF CURRICULAR MATERIALS
(3) *Bitty Bops—Toddlers* music teachers should be thoroughly familiar with all the songs and activities so that Toddlers may be taught according to their developmental and response stages.

    TODDLERS SONGS COLLECTION: These categorical songs and activities, indexed by music activity categories, are compiled and field-tested by an experienced pre-K12 music teacher for more than a decade of teaching at this age level. **(See Document 14.)**

    MUSIC TOGETHER SONG COLLECTIONS: From Ken Guilmartin and Dr. Lillian Levinowitz, pre-K12 music experts at Rowan University. **(See Document 15.)**

Tambourine Song Collection	Sticks Song Collection
Fiddle Song Collection	Flute Song Collection
Triangle Song Collection	Summer Songs 1
Drum Song Collection	Summer Songs 2
Bongos Song Collection	Summer Songs 3
Maracas Song Collection	Babies
Bells Song Collection	Family Favorites Songbook for Teachers

    MUSIC PLAY: BOOK 1: From Dr. Gordon and his associates at Temple University and surrounding areas, this music book is created based on the music learning sequence Gordon research for pre-K12ers. **(See Document 16.)**

NICHOL'S WORTH: VOLUMES 1-2-3-4: A great collection of fun and humorous songs. These are witty, folk-like songs in four volumes, featuring all combinations of Meters (duple, triple, and multi-metric combined); Modes (Major, Minor, Dorian, Mixolydian, Phrygian, Lydian, and multi-tonal); in vocal textures (unison, combinable songs, partner songs, ostinatos, countermelodies, and rounds) that many other song collections neglect to include. **(See Document 17.)** (For the much-neglected Locrian mode, see the Knauss Music Curriculum, Book 1, pp. 50, 82-84. All modes may be sung in canon, see Knauss Music Curriculum, Book 3, pp. 18-20. For the Locrian mode, transpose the canon to the scale notes B to B: Ti-Do-Re-Mi-Fa-So-La-Ti.)

THE BOOK OF MOVEMENT EXPLORATION: CAN YOU MOVE LIKE THIS? Dr. John Feierabend has many years of research and experience with pre-K12 music teaching as well as expertly certified in the Kódaly music education approach. **(See Document 18.)**

FIRST STEPS IN CLASSICAL MUSIC: KEEPING THE BEAT! Dr. John Feierabend compiled an accompanying CD to the above book featuring many great classical works for children's exposure to classical styles. **(See Document 18.)**

TODDLERS MUSIC LESSON PLANS

(4) *Bitty Bops—Toddlers* music teachers need to be familiar with all of the above information, songs, and activities, to the point of having them memorized so that they naturally flow out of the music teacher in smooth, well-transitioned, dove-tailed music lessons. See the lesson plan instructions and example music lesson plans for dovetailing and planning a balanced presentation and exposure to all Active Participations, Rhythm and Tonal Patterns, Song Categories, Meters, and Modes. **(See Document 13.)**

Contents for *Bitty Bops—Toddlers*
(Documents 10-18)

                                                                                                               Page

Document 10: How to Use *Bitty Bops—Toddlers* Music Curriculum 62

Document 11: Toddlers Lesson Structure and Activities Explained 65

Document 12: How Toddlers Learn Music 67

Document 13: Toddlers Music Lesson Plans 70

Document 14: Toddlers Songs Notebook Index 79

Document 15: Toddlers Music Together Books Index... 88

Document 16: Toddlers Music Play Book Index 103

Document 17: Toddlers Nichol's Worth Books Index... 107

Document 18: Toddlers Movement Exploration and Keeping the Beat Index 112

Toddlers Classes & Activities Explained
Ages 2 thru 3

"Cardinal" Rules that must never be broken or neglected when teaching pre-K12 music classes:

1. Every song must have movement on the steady beat (except for purposeful interpretive movements). Always plan your movements. Also, copy any students' spontaneous movements.
2. All movements must exhibit a steady beat.
3. Male and female teachers alike must use their head voices so that the students learn to match in their light head voices. When all students are securely in tune, then the male teacher may use his lower voice and be certain that the students are aware of the octave transfer.
4. The teacher should never play an instrument to have students match pitches, because the transfer gap in timbre from instrument to voice is too wide. The teacher must always use voice to voice.
5. At the end of every singing song, the teacher sings the "Sol-Do" of the song with hand motions—palms pointing down at chest level (Sol) and ending on the floor or waist level (Do). Pause for two seconds after the Sol, to allow for students to respond if they wish with the Do.

Each Toddlers Lesson Plan should contain the following, depending on class length:

1. Bouncing or lap song / stationary movement
2. Finger play / body awareness songs and activities
3. Large gross motor activity / traveling movement—possibly using manipulatives, such as toy horses, hoops, scarves
4. Steady beat activities to utilize each of the following instruments—(sticks, drums, jingles, shakers, scarves)
5. Songs focused on vocal responses / call and response activities (resonator bars)
6. Focused listening sounds
7. Rhythmic and tonal patterns, both simple and complex
8. Group dance activity
9. From one music activity to the next, music concepts dovetailed (see Lesson Plan chart).
10. For the music learning stages of toddlers, see IMITATION stages in the chart of How Toddlers Learn Music (see Document 12).
11. Each class should contain approximately 12-14 songs including hello/goodbye songs, dependent on time length of class. The use of the word parent in the follow paragraphs denotes caregiver, babysitter, family relative, or anyone who regularly brings the toddler to each class.

Repetition. Repetition the most important aspect of learning in early childhood music. Songs are repeated from week to week, but varied with different instruments and movements. The majority of each class is repeated familiar songs and activities, with only a few being introduced as new. When new ones are consistently repeated, they too become familiar.

Actions Not Explanations. The teacher begins each class with singing, ends with singing, and even sings all 4-word-or-less instructions between activities (only if instructions are absolutely needed). In preschool ages, children do not learn with linguistic explanations—they learn experientially. Only parents need explanations, such as the preschool stages of learning (see IMITATION stages in chart of How Toddlers Learn Music (see Document 12), or reminders why their participation is the superior modeling for their toddler. When parents need explanations or reminders that they are active participants all the time, provide these apart from the flow of the lesson. Parents should sing every song the same as the teacher, because toddlers need the emotional connection of the parent voice that they have been listening to since before they were born. Music is learned in the same way as language (Suzuki's "mother tongue" concept). So it is because we speak to toddlers, regardless of their ability to answer or understand, to immerse them in unlimited exposure. In this way, toddlers will acquire the sounds and rhythms. Usually beginning in Kindergarten or after they begin to read and write in the language.

Smooth Transitions. When moving from song to song, either sing a transition melodic phrase, or a clean-up song. Do not speak instructions. Keep the music ongoing. Think about what is coming next and prepare toddlers and parents for the activity with movement to do together. "March with me," or "caw like a crow," or just jump right into the next song or activity. Don't stop the music, but rather keep songs flowing from one to the next. If a child does not want to "clean up," they will eventually copy the others. When you, the teacher, give out the next object for the next activity, you can trade them objects without saying a word or bringing attention to their negative behavior. In this way, always promote a positive atmosphere.

Playing Not Performing. Real learning that will stick, will happen when toddlers feel comfortable in their learning environment, when there is repetition, and when they are emotionally connected to the activity through laughter and enjoyment. Growing a relationship with toddlers can happen through music class, which of course is inherently fun, but a child will also naturally gravitate to someone who will "play" with them. An effective early childhood teacher is one who has a playful spirit and is thoroughly animated. Children learn through play and are naturally playful beings. They will respond to adults who are authentically silly right along with them. Teachers need to find that playful spirit that feels natural to them.

Acceptance Without Expectations. Children are different learners. Some are active participants and some do not participate at all but they are absorbing the class and its activities like a sponge, regardless of what they are doing on the exterior. What they do in class, most likely they will imitate at home where they are most comfortable. We take the children, where they are, and whatever type of learner they are, and accept them as they are. Early childhood music education, informal music education, is not at all like formal music education in K-12, where responses are expected. The teacher must be aware that participation or responses may or may not happen depending on the learning stage of the toddlers (see IMITATION stages in chart of How Toddlers Learn Music (see Document 12).

Parent Participation. Parents should be reminded that they are to be their toddler's example. Parents must be involved, not sitting or standing as silent observers outside the activity circle. Toddlers need to see that their parents value music and that they lead by modeling, showing the joy of music even when the toddler is not participating. Parent socializing should not happen during class, and should be addressed either through an initial handout explaining class procedure and parental expectations, or verbal reminders. Remind the parents to turn their "talking" voices off as they enter the room. Parents may also need to be reminded that the music curriculum is developmentally geared to the preschool child so repetition is a key component. Toddlers are emotionally connected to their parents and their voices, so when modeling, remind parents that it doesn't matter how well or perfectly they sound. It is primarily the fact that it is THEIR sound their toddler will respond to and connect with. This ensures that the best learning will happen!

How Toddlers Learn Music

Gordon, E.E. (2003). *A music learning theory for newborn and young children.* Chicago, IL: GIA Publications, Inc. ISBN: 1-57999-259-5.

"Audiation takes place when one hears and comprehends music silently, the sound of the music no longer being or never having been physically present. In contrast, aural perception takes place when one hears music when its sound is physically present." (p. 25)

"Audition is to music what thought is to language. Audiating while you are performing music is like thinking while you are speaking, and audiating while listening to music is like thinking about what persons have said and are saying as you are listening to them speak." (p. 25)

"Audiation is the basis of music aptitude." (p. 25)

Music learning continues for Ages 2-4 to 3-5 with the IMITATION stages, after sequentially developing through the ACCULTURATION stages. (See the following IMITATION stages.)

TYPES	CHILD'S RESPONSES	TEACHER'S INTERACTION
2. IMITATION: Ages 2-4 to 3-5: participates with conscious thought focused primarily on the environment (p. 41) IMITATION is children first learning to discern differences in their responses to others, and second what are accurate responses and what are not. First, children become able to discern with accuracy what they have heard when they are not imitating. Children may realize that their own singing, chanting, and movements are not accurate imitations of others. Second, children attempt to move beyond their personal world of music and into the music world at large. They gain experience in recognizing patterns performed for them and attempt accurate imitations in response. Imitation has two sub stages of development: (a) children become aware of sameness and difference between what they are singing or chanting and what another child or adult is performing, and (b) children begin to imitate with some precision the tonal patterns and rhythm patterns that another child or adult is singing or chanting. Children become aware of the way they are breathing and moving their bodies in connection with their singing of tonal patterns and chanting of rhythm patterns, and children consciously learn	2.A. SHEDDING EGOCENTRICITY: Recognizes that movement and babble do not match the sounds of music in the environment (p. 41) Children make their initial transition from preparatory audiation and music babble to audiation. They become aware of sameness and difference between what they are singing or chanting and what another child or adult is performing. (p. 44) CHILD'S RESPONSES OR REACTIONS TO MUSIC: Child recognizes that his/her movement and babble do not match the sounds of music in the environment. Child will attempt tonal and rhythm patterns, not necessarily with accuracy, and with no coordination among breathing, moving, and singing. At first, there may be no indication that the child realizes his/her pattern is different from the model. Child's tonal pattern may contain the resting tone or the dominant pitch. When child realizes that what she is performing is different from the model, (s)he does so with an "audiation stare."	TEACHER'S INTERACTION WITH CHILD'S RESPONSES: Continue with structured informal guidance during tonal and rhythmic Imitation pattern guidance and classroom activities. Perform tonal Imitation patterns that feature the resting tone and a perfect 5th above or perfect 4th below, if the range of the pattern accommodates child's singing and initial audiation range. Continue to model a deep, full breath preceding each tonal pattern. Encourage child to respond by changing your facial expressions, using gestures, and moving with continuous flow that emphasizes differences in weight, space, and time. As a child responds inaccurately to your tonal or rhythm pattern, use his/her inaccurate pattern to begin a pattern dialogue with him/her so that (s)he may learn the process of imitation. Perform four-macro beat Imitation patterns with expression and conversation-like inflection, mixing staccato and legato articulation and using changes in dynamics. Return frequently to the original tonal and rhythm Imitation patterns. If a child performs and "audiation stare," move to the next Stage 2.B. Encourage spontaneous songs, chants, and movements created by child. Continue to perform music in a variety of tonalities and meters while moving with continuous flow.

	2.B. BREAKING THE CODE:	TEACHER'S INTERACTION WITH CHILD'S RESPONSES:
to coordinate with some precision their singing and chanting of tonal patterns and rhythm patterns with their breathing and the weight and flow of their body movements.	Imitates with some precision the sounds of music in the environment, specifically tonal patterns and rhythm patterns (p. 41) Children begin to imitate with some precision the tonal patterns and rhythm patterns that another child or adult is singing or chanting. (p. 45) CHILD'S RESPONSES OR REACTIONS TO MUSIC: Child imitates with some precision the sounds of music in the environment. Child has indicated the (s)he realized his/her tonal patterns were different from the adult's. Child is continuing to learn about imitation by engaging in pattern dialogue. Child's tonal or rhythm patterns may or may not be precisely like the adults.	Continue structured informal guidance during tonal and rhythmic Imitation pattern guidance and classroom activities. Begin monitoring specific and individual differences among children's tonal and rhythmic responses. Sing arpeggioed tonal Imitation and Assimilation patterns. Continue to model a deep, full breath preceding each tonal pattern. Continue assisting child in discovering the process of imitation by creating a tonal pattern dialogue using his/her inaccurate patterns. Do this with rhythm pattern dialogues as well. Frequently return to original tonal or rhythm patterns. Encourage child to imitate you by using facial expressions, gestures, and movement with continuous flow that include weight, space, and time. Encourage spontaneous songs, chants, and movements created by child. Continue to perform music in a variety of tonalities and meters while moving with continuous flow.

Gordon, E.E. (2003). *A music learning theory for newborn and young children*. Chicago, IL: GIA Publications, Inc. ISBN: 1-57999-259-5. (summarized from pp. 41, 44-45).

Toddlers Music Lesson Plans
Guidelines for Planning

(1) Whatever you choose as the "Hello Song" and "Goodbye Song" for the first class of the semester, keep those songs consistent for the whole semester. Change the "Hello" and "Goodbye" songs to different ones for a following semester.

(2) Follow careful Dovetailing of music concepts from activity to activity so that something remains familiar from activity to activity in each lesson—thus controlling the number of music concepts that are new from activity to activity. Also carefully track the repetition and changing of music concepts down the column. (See the Infant Lesson Plans, Document 03, for how they are repeated or "dovetailed" from activity to activity.)

(3) Carefully plan the number of familiar activities, as opposed to new activities, from lesson to lesson. Repeat a majority of familiar songs from the previous lesson(s) and use a small number of new songs. (See the arrows that point forward into the next lesson plan. These arrows indicate the songs that are carried as familiar over into the next lesson plan.)

(4) Be sure to include something of Listening, Singing, Chanting, Moving, Playing, Performing, Creating, and Improvising in some way throughout the progress of each lesson. (See the third column labeled Dovetailing of Mode / Meter / Specialty.)

(5) Choose 3-4 Duple and Triple Rhythms and insert into the Lesson Plan where appropriate. Choose 3-4 Major and Minor Tonal Patterns and insert into the Lesson Plan where appropriate. Chant on neutral syllable "ba" for rhythm and sing on neutral syllable "nu" or "loo" for tonal. Perform the rhythm and tonal patterns looking directly at the toddler. Pause a second or two after each to give the toddler time to respond if (s)he desires. Whatever response is given, immediately copy it back to the toddler. (These rhythms and tonal patterns are found in the Knauss Music Curriculum, Book 1A.)

(6) Plan for music activities that are at the Toddlers' level as well as music that is beyond the Toddlers' level, the same as parents use single words and short phrases to their toddlers, as well as speak adult-level large coherent paragraphs with complex words and sentence structures.

(7) Include listening and moving to an instrumental selection in each lesson—whether popular, classical, cultural, or whatever.

(8) Because music potential is genius level at birth, and slowly declines from there, always provide the toddlers with the greatest exposure to all kinds and levels and complexity of music—nothing is outside their exposure, absorption, and imitation abilities at this age.

Tracking the Content of Toddlers Lesson Plans

When planning the sequence of each next lesson from the one before, the goal is for an evenly varied musical exposure and experience across each class semester.

	Active Participations				Rhythm & Tonal Patterns			Songs							Meters			Modes						
								Song Categories																
	Singing / Chanting	Moving	Playing / Performing	Creating / Improvising	Duple Rhythm Patterns	Triple Rhythm Patterns	Tonal Patterns	Hello / Goodbye Songs	Bouncing Song / Lap Song	Finger Play / Body Awareness	Large Gross Motor Activity with Movement	Steady Beat Activity with Instruments	Vocal Response / Call and Response Activity	Group Dance Activity	Duple Meter	Triple Meter	Unusual Meter	Major (Ionian)	Minor (Aeolian)	Mixolydian	Dorian	Lydian	Phrygian	Locrian
Lesson 1																								
Lesson 2																								
Lesson 3																								
Lesson 4																								
Lesson 5																								
Lesson 6																								
Lesson 7																								
Lesson 8																								
Lesson 9																								
Lesson 10																								
Lesson 11																								
Lesson 12																								
Lesson 13																								
Lesson 14																								
Lesson 15																								
TOTALS (Goal is for an evenly varied musical exposure and experience across each class semester)																								

Bitty Bops—Toddlers—Document 13

Toddlers Music Lesson Plan 1

Choose 3-4 Duple and Triple Rhythms and insert into the Lesson Plan where appropriate.
Choose 3-4 Major and Minor Tonal Patterns and insert into the Lesson Plan where appropriate.

CATEGORY	MATERIALS	DOVETAILING OF MODE / METER / SPECIALTY	ACTIVITY
Hello Song	"Hello Song" Music Together—Sticks Song Collection, p. 13	Major Duple Singing & Pat / Clap the Duple Meter	Sit in a circle and sway back and forth gently on the macrobeats—perform steady beats
Bouncing Song / Lap Song			
Finger Play / Body Awareness			
Large Gross Motor Activity / Traveling Movement & Hoops			
Steady Beat Activity with Instruments			
Vocal Response / Call and Respond Activity			
Group Dance Activity			
Goodbye Song	"Goodbye, So Long, Farewell" by Ken Guilmartin Music Together—Sticks, p. 45	Major Triple Swaying & Pat / Clap / Clap the Triple Meter	Back to sitting in a circle—use each of the toddler's and parent's names to sing goodbye—sway a goodbye hand to the triple meter

(There are only 8 activities above; 12-14 are to be planned by repeating categories.)

Bitty Bops—Toddlers—Document 13

Toddlers Music Lesson Plan 2

Choose 3-4 Duple and Triple Rhythms and insert into the Lesson Plan where appropriate.
Choose 3-4 Major and Minor Tonal Patterns and insert into the Lesson Plan where appropriate.

CATEGORY	MATERIALS	DOVETAILING OF MODE / METER / SPECIALTY	ACTIVITY
Hello Song	"Hello Song" Music Together—Sticks Song Collection, p. 13	Major Duple Singing & Pat / Clap the Duple Meter	Sit in a circle and sway back and forth gently on the macrobeats—perform steady beats
Bouncing Song / Lap Song			
Finger Play / Body Awareness			
Large Gross Motor Activity / Traveling Movement & Hoops			
Steady Beat Activity with Instruments			
Vocal Response / Call and Respond Activity			
Group Dance Activity			
Goodbye Song	"Goodbye, So Long, Farewell" by Ken Guilmartin Music Together—Sticks, p. 45	Major Triple Swaying & Pat / Clap / Clap the Triple Meter	Back to sitting in a circle—use each of the toddler's and parent's names to sing goodbye—sway a goodbye hand to the triple meter

(There are only 8 activities above; 12-14 are to be planned by repeating categories.)

Toddlers Music Lesson Plan 3

Choose 3-4 Duple and Triple Rhythms and insert into the Lesson Plan where appropriate.
Choose 3-4 Major and Minor Tonal Patterns and insert into the Lesson Plan where appropriate.

CATEGORY	MATERIALS	DOVETAILING OF MODE / METER / SPECIALTY	ACTIVITY
Hello Song	"Hello Song" Music Together—Sticks Song Collection, p. 13	Major Duple Singing & Pat / Clap the Duple Meter	Sit in a circle and sway back and forth gently on the macrobeats—perform steady beats
Bouncing Song / Lap Song			
Finger Play / Body Awareness			
Large Gross Motor Activity / Traveling Movement & Hoops			
Steady Beat Activity with Instruments			
Vocal Response / Call and Respond Activity			
Group Dance Activity			
Goodbye Song	"Goodbye, So Long, Farewell" by Ken Guilmartin Music Together—Sticks, p. 45	Major Triple Swaying & Pat / Clap / Clap the Triple Meter	Back to sitting in a circle—use each of the toddler's and parent's names to sing goodbye—sway a goodbye hand to the triple meter

(There are only 8 activities above; 12-14 are to be planned by repeating categories.)

Toddlers Music Lesson Plan 4

Choose 3-4 Duple and Triple Rhythms and insert into the Lesson Plan where appropriate.
Choose 3-4 Major and Minor Tonal Patterns and insert into the Lesson Plan where appropriate.

CATEGORY	MATERIALS	DOVETAILING OF MODE / METER / SPECIALTY	ACTIVITY
Hello Song	"Hello Song" Music Together—Sticks Song Collection, p. 13	Major Duple Singing & Pat / Clap the Duple Meter	Sit in a circle and sway back and forth gently on the macrobeats—perform steady beats
Bouncing Song / Lap Song			
Finger Play / Body Awareness			
Large Gross Motor Activity / Traveling Movement & Hoops			
Steady Beat Activity with Instruments			
Vocal Response / Call and Respond Activity			
Group Dance Activity			
Goodbye Song	"Goodbye, So Long, Farewell" by Ken Guilmartin Music Together—Sticks, p. 45	Major Triple Swaying & Pat / Clap / Clap the Triple Meter	Back to sitting in a circle—use each of the toddler's and parent's names to sing goodbye—sway a goodbye hand to the triple meter

(There are only 8 activities above; 12-14 are to be planned by repeating categories.)

Toddlers Music Lesson Plan 5

Choose 3-4 Duple and Triple Rhythms and insert into the Lesson Plan where appropriate.
Choose 3-4 Major and Minor Tonal Patterns and insert into the Lesson Plan where appropriate.

CATEGORY	MATERIALS	DOVETAILING OF MODE / METER / SPECIALTY	ACTIVITY
Hello Song	"Hello Song" Music Together—Sticks Song Collection, p. 13	Major Duple Singing & Pat / Clap the Duple Meter	Sit in a circle and sway back and forth gently on the macrobeats—perform steady beats
Bouncing Song / Lap Song			
Finger Play / Body Awareness			
Large Gross Motor Activity / Traveling Movement & Hoops			
Steady Beat Activity with Instruments			
Vocal Response / Call and Respond Activity			
Group Dance Activity			
Goodbye Song	"Goodbye, So Long, Farewell" by Ken Guilmartin Music Together—Sticks, p. 45	Major Triple Swaying & Pat / Clap / Clap the Triple Meter	Back to sitting in a circle—use each of the toddler's and parent's names to sing goodbye—sway a goodbye hand to the triple meter

(There are only 8 activities above; 12-14 are to be planned by repeating categories.)

Toddlers Music Lesson Plan 6

Choose 3-4 Duple and Triple Rhythms and insert into the Lesson Plan where appropriate.
Choose 3-4 Major and Minor Tonal Patterns and insert into the Lesson Plan where appropriate.

CATEGORY	MATERIALS	DOVETAILING OF MODE / METER / SPECIALTY	ACTIVITY
Hello Song	"Hello Song" Music Together—Sticks Song Collection, p. 13	Major Duple Singing & Pat / Clap the Duple Meter	Sit in a circle and sway back and forth gently on the macrobeats—perform steady beats
Bouncing Song / Lap Song			
Finger Play / Body Awareness			
Large Gross Motor Activity / Traveling Movement & Hoops			
Steady Beat Activity with Instruments			
Vocal Response / Call and Respond Activity			
Group Dance Activity			
Goodbye Song	"Goodbye, So Long, Farewell" by Ken Guilmartin Music Together—Sticks, p. 45	Major Triple Swaying & Pat / Clap / Clap the Triple Meter	Back to sitting in a circle—use each of the toddler's and parent's names to sing goodbye—sway a goodbye hand to the triple meter

(There are only 8 activities above; 12-14 are to be planned by repeating categories.)

Toddlers Music Lesson Plan 7

Choose 3-4 Duple and Triple Rhythms and insert into the Lesson Plan where appropriate.
Choose 3-4 Major and Minor Tonal Patterns and insert into the Lesson Plan where appropriate.

CATEGORY	MATERIALS	DOVETAILING OF MODE / METER / SPECIALTY	ACTIVITY
Hello Song	"Hello Song" Music Together—Sticks Song Collection, p. 13	Major Duple Singing & Pat / Clap the Duple Meter	Sit in a circle and sway back and forth gently on the macrobeats—perform steady beats
Bouncing Song / Lap Song			
Finger Play / Body Awareness			
Large Gross Motor Activity / Traveling Movement & Hoops			
Steady Beat Activity with Instruments			
Vocal Response / Call and Respond Activity			
Group Dance Activity			
Goodbye Song	"Goodbye, So Long, Farewell" by Ken Guilmartin Music Together—Sticks, p. 45	Major Triple Swaying & Pat / Clap / Clap the Triple Meter	Back to sitting in a circle—use each of the toddler's and parent's names to sing goodbye—sway a goodbye hand to the triple meter

(There are only 8 activities above; 12-14 are to be planned by repeating categories.)

Toddlers Songs Collection
Indexed by Music Activity
Ages 2 thru 3

NOTE: The follow songs are organized by suggested activity categories. The music for them may be found in well-known publications or on the Internet.

Lap Songs / Bouncing Songs. Each lesson should contain songs where the toddler is bounced in the parent's lap to the steady beat of the music. Different positions can be used when participating in bouncing activities where the toddler can face outwards towards the other toddlers in the circle or the toddler faces the parent. Some songs may include surprises, such as where the toddler is lifted from under the arms into the air or supporting under their legs and bottoms to lift them up while you roll back as to "whoa" the horses. This always produces giggles and smiles. In this activity the toddler feels and hears that steady beat internally and externally while enjoying the bonding and closeness of being in their parent's lap and having the parent's undivided attention. Movement stimulates and charges the brain as toddlers learn through play; moving and being moved in the environment around them.

Allee Galloo (Music Together-Triangle) CD#21 Bounce and swing back with them in lap on "whee" .... Triple / Major

Ally Bally (Music Together-Triangle) CD#19 .... Duple / Major

Bim Bam (Music Together-Maracas) rock & tap steady beat .... Duple / Minor

Horsey, Horsey (www.youtube.com/watch?v=kfPKWCITnps) .... Triple / Major

Jack and Jill (nursery rhyme) (http://www.youtube.com/watch?v=8RoAJqcn9E4) Roll back after broke his crown .... Triple / Major

Jack Be Nimble (Music Together-Maracas) .... Triple Rhythmic Chant

Li'L 'Liza Jane (Music Together-Bongs) CD#21 .... Duple / Major / Partner Songs

See How I'm Jumping (Music Together-Bongos) Sing Bouncing & Rocking instead .... Duple / Minor

She'll Be Comin' Round The Mountain (Music Together-Bongos).......... Duple / Major

Shoo Fly (Music Together-Bongo) CD#17 .... Duple / Major

Sweet Potato (Music Together-Babies) (www.youtube.com/watch?v=0cr1dczj-yM) .... Duple / Major

Trot to Grandma's House (Music Together-Babies) .... Duple / Major

Trot, Trot, Trot (Bouncing song) .... Duple / Major

William Tell's Ride (Music Together-Maracas) .... Duple / Major & Minor

Bitty Bops—Toddlers—Document 14

Finger Play / Body Awareness. Finger play activities allow for fine motor exercises and language development growth opportunities. These songs/poems are more stationary and can lead into songs having to do with the same subject matter, such as rocking songs or lullabies with resonator bars. These are taught by singing first as an example and asking the children to join them or take out their "turtles" or whatever the finger play is about. The children should be the teacher's mirror as the teacher sings the song and asks them where their "body parts" are so they can tap them, etc. Parents should mirror the teacher as the song is sung, as parents show toddlers where their "body parts" are so they can tap them, etc.

Clap Your Hands (Music Together-Drums) Tap body parts then add instruments ....Duple / Mixolydian on D

Deedle Deedle Dumpling (Music Together-Bells) Act out song verses .... Duple / Dorian

Eensy, Weensey Spider (Music Together-Bongo) CD#15 .... Triple (or Compound Duple) / Major

Five Little Mice (Music Together-Maracas) Then use instruments to be mice scampering away ....Duple Rhythmic Chant

Head, Shoulders, Knees, and Toes .... Duple or Triple Rhythmic Chant, or if sung Duple / Major

Here Is Bunny (Music Together-Triangle) CD#31 First use fingers then get hoops—be a hopping bunny...Triple Rhythmic Chant

Here Is The Beehive (Music Together-Fiddle)............................Triple Rhythmic Chant

I've Got The Rhythm In My Head (Music Together-Fiddle) .... Duple / Major

Open and Shut Them (Music Together-Bongos) CD#4 .... Duple / Major

Russian Folk Song (Music Together-Maracas) Also known as "May There Always Be Sunshine" (rocking song) .... Duple / Major

Sneak and Peek (Music Together-Drums) scarves .... Duple / Dorian on D

Ten Fingers (Music Together-Triangle).......................................Duple Rhythmic Chant

The Snail and The Mouse (Music Together-Drums) ....Duple Rhythmic Chant

There's A Cobbler (Music Together-Drums) sticks ....Duple Rhythmic Chant

This Little Light of Mine (Music Together-Fiddle).................................. Duple / Major

This Old Man (Music Together-Bongos) CD#8.. Duple / Major

Two Little Blackbirds (Music Together-Triangle) CD#26......................... Duple / Major

Large Gross Motor Activity / Traveling Movement and Hoops. Movement songs are active and have children up and moving. They will improve a child's coordination, balance, and spatial awareness. These songs can be songs about different types of movement such as jumping, marching, twirling, or could be songs that can use hoops to jump into or crawl through. These songs can be sung first stationary or bouncing to the beat, or using body percussion, and then sung with traveling movements or manipulatives, such as horses, scarves, etc.

A Ram Sam Sam (Music Together-Fiddle) .... Duple / Major

All Around The Kitchen (Music Together-Maracas)
.... Duple / Three classic blues forms of 12-bar, 8-bar, & 16-bar on A Minor

City Blues (Music Together-Bongos) CD#2 use with hoops
.... Duple / Major

Crawdad (Music Together-Fiddle) .... Duple / Major

Dame Get Up travel movement / hoops .... Triple / Minor

Drummers Marching (Music Together-Triangle) CD#23 .... Triple / Minor

Goin' To Boston (Music Together-Fiddle) w/ hoops .... Duple / Mixolydian on C

Hop Ol' Squirrel (Music Together-Maracas) do the motions of squirrel before adding instruments .... Duple / Major

Jumpin' Josie (Music Together-Maracas) .... Duple / Do Pentatonic on D

Ladybug (Music Together-Triangle) CD#17 movement improvisation
.... Triple / Dorian Implied

Merry Go Round (Music Together-Babies) use with hoops or stick horses
.... Triple / Minor

My Lady Wind (Music Together-Bells) scarves / hoops .... Duple / Major

Riding In A Buggy   hoops .... Duple / Major

Round and Round the Haystack hoops / baby finger play
.... Triple Rhythmic Chant

Sally Go Round The Sun hoops .... Triple / Major

Santa Maloney (hoops / circle dance) .... Triple / Major

See How I'm Jumping (Music Together-Bongos) CD#7 can use with hoops
.... Duple / Minor

See The Pony Galloping scarves .... Triple / Major

This Train (Music Together-Drums) .... Duple / Dorian on D (Countermelodies)

Tingalayo (Music Together-Babies) movement or stick horses
(www.youtube.com/watch?v=trCOfgwikjY) .... Duple / Major

Train Is a-Comin' (Music Together-Bongos) CD#12 shakers .... Duple / Major

Train To The City (Music Together-Maracas) make a train around the room
.... Duple / Major

Two Little Kitty Cats (Music Together-Bells) hoop .... Duple / Minor

Walk All Around / Tap On Your Sticks movement / sticks .... Duple / Major

William Tell's Ride (Music Together-Maracas) (Music Together-Babies) ride with stick ponies / bounce / use with scarves as reigns for horses (www.youtube.com/watch?v=xoHECVnQC7A) .... Duple / Major and Minor

Steady Beat Activities Utilizing Instruments (sticks, drums, shakers, resonator bars, jingles, scarves). Plan for 2-3 songs for the children to hear the steady beat and use instruments to match that beat. The song is introduced by singing first and using body percussion to illustrate the beats. Then these movements are transferred to playing steady beat instruments. The teacher always models the beats as the children simultaneously mirror. The children can use sticks in varying ways to keep the beat to a song with or without words.

A Ram Sam Sam (Music Together-Fiddle) .... Duple / Major

Allee Galloo (Music Together-Triangle) CD#21 use scarves to beat & throw / catch .... Triple / Major

Apples and Cherries (Music Together-Fiddle) .... Duple / Major / Tonal Round

Baa, Baa Black Sheep .... Duple / Major

Biddy Biddy (Music Together-Drums) shakers or jingles .... Duple / Major

Bim Bam (Music Together-Maracas) .... Duple / Minor

Bongo Jam (Music Together-Bongo) CD#14 instrumental instrument jam .... Duple / Major / Instrumental Play Along

Breezes (Music Together-Triangle) CD#12 dance free style with scarves .... Triple / Mixolydian on D

Canoe Song (Music Together-Bongo) CD#20 drums or sticks .... Duple / Minor

Clap Your Hands (Music Together-Drums) .... Duple / Mixolydian on D

Drummers Marching (Music Together-Triangle) CD#23 .... Triple / Minor

Dum Ditty Dum (Music Together-Flutes) drums /sticks .... Duple / Major

Frere Jacques (Music Together-Maracas)
.... Duple / Major / Vocal and Instrumental Ostinatos

Hey Lolly, Lolly (Music Together-Flutes) sticks or scarves .... Duple / Major

Hop Ol' Squirrel (Music Together-Maracas) drum .... Duple / Major

I Can Hammer sticks / bells.. Triple / Major

I Had A Little Frog (Music Together-Flutes) drum .... Duple Rhythmic Chant

I Hear Some Knockin' / Peas Porridge Hot drum echo rhythm patterns
.... Duple / Major

I'm A Bell (Music Together-Maracas) .... Triple / Minor

I'm Gonna Play Today (Music Together-Bells) scarves / dance .... Duple / Major

I'm Hiding (Music Together-Triangle) rap with scarves .... Duple Rhythmic Chant

I've Been Working On the Railroad (Music Together-Flutes) shakers
.... Duple / Major

I've Got The Rhythm In My Head (Music Together-Fiddle) .... Duple / Major

Jim Along Josie (Music Together-Flutes) sticks .... Duple / Major

Little Johnny Brown (Music Together-Bongos) CD#19 scarves
.... Duple / Natural Minor

Mr. Rabbit (Music Together-Bells) jingles .... Duple / Major

My Lady Wind (Music Together-Bells) scarves .... Duple / Major

Noble Duke of York drums / circle dance .... Duple / Major

Nothin' Blues (Music Together-Triangle) CD#2 steady beat with shakers or other percussion .... Duple / Major in Blues Style

Peas Porridge Hot (Music Together-Maracas) .... Duple Rhythmic Chant

Rain Song (Music Together-Triangle) CD#9 sticks or drums
.... Duple / Dorian on D

Riding In A Buggy drums or hoops .... Duple / Major

Shake Those 'Simmons Down (Music Together-Flutes) shakers .... Duple / Major

She'll Be Comin' Round The Mountain (Music Together-Bongos) use instruments for special effects .... Duple / Major

Ten Fingers (Music Together-Triangle) jingles .... Duple Rhythmic Chant

The Bells of Westminster (Music Together-Bells) jingles
.... Duple / Major / Round and Countermelodies

The Snail and The Mouse (Music Together-Drums) .... Duple Rhythmic Chant

The Wiggle Song scarves .... Triple / Major

There's A Cobbler (Music Together-Drums) sticks .... Duple Rhythmic Chant

There's a Little Wheel-a-Turning (Music Together-Flutes) jingles .... Duple / Major

This Old Man (Music Together-Bongos) CD#8 different percussion instruments
.... Duple / Major

This Train (Music Together-Drums) shakers
.... Duple / Dorian on D (Countermelodies)

Train Is a-Comin' (Music Together-Bongos) CD#12 shakers .... Duple / Major

Train To The City (Music Together-Maracas) shakers .... Duple / Major

Two Little Blackbirds (Music Together-Triangle) CD#26 shakers, jingles, or scarves .... Duple / Major

Wake Up you Lazy Bones jingles.. Duple / Major

Walk All Around/Tap On Your Sticks   sticks / drums .... Duple / Major

Walking Through the Woods (Music Together-Bongos) CD#6 scarves .... Triple / Minor

Went to Visit the Farm resonator bars / call & response .... Duple / Major

When Johnny Comes Marching Home .... Triple / Minor

Who's That? (Music Together-Babies/Bells) scarves / drums .... Duple / Major

William Had Seven Sons shakers .... Duple / Minor

Vocal Response / Call and Response Activities. These songs and activities encourage a response from the child, but responses may or may not be given, depending on the learning stage of the child (see IMITATION stages in the Chart of How Preschoolers Learn Music). The teacher is not to require any response. These activities will create opportunities for the nonverbal or shy child to use his/her speaking voice, as well as develop the child's singing voice. The songs are sung first as an example and the response is taught by rote. The activity continues with reminding the parent to be the response example for the child, and praising any response from any child. Once the songs are learned and introduced, resonator bars can be added to keep the steady beat using notes from the song's harmony. These songs or activities not only include sung responses, but also responding with farm animal sounds or tonal patterns, depending on what the teacher first presents to be echoed.

Bird Song (Music Together-Triangle) CD#6 resonator bars .... Triple / Phrygian on C

Bow, Wow, Wow resonators bells... Duple / Major

By 'n' By (Music Together-Bells) jingles, children sing their number as a counted star .... Duple / Major

Doodle (Music Together-Maracas) add resonator bells
.... Duple (Swing) / Dorian on D

Dum Ditty Dum (Music Together-Flutes) resonator bars, Children echo each line as you sing it, Use verses written.. Duple / Major

Fireworks (Music Together-Bongos) CD#9 vocal exploration and scarves
....Triple Rhythmic Chant

I Hear Some Knockin' drum echo rhythm patterns .... Duple / Major

John The Rabbit (Music Together-Drum) .... Duple / Major

Li'L 'Liza Jane / Funga Alafia (Music Together-Bongs) CD#21 vocal with resonator bars .... Duple / Major / Partner Songs

Little Green Frog guiro, sticks & sing / play on tone bells, frog sounds
.... Duple / Major

No More Pie (Music Together-Fiddle) vocal with resonator bells
.... Duple / Minor Blues

Old Blue (Music Together-Triangle) CD#27 .... Duple / Mixolydian on D

Peas Porridge Hot (Music Together-Maracas) .... Duple Rhythmic Chant

Sandpiper (Music Together-Flutes) rewritten as "The Echo" (resonator bars)
.... Duple / Major

She'll Be Comin' Round The Mountain (Music Together-Bongos) vocal special effects
.... Duple / Major

Twinkle, Twinkle (resonator bars or little choir bells) sing and play their bell note
.... Duple / Major

Went to Visit the Farm resonator bars / call & response .... Duple / Major

When Ducks Get Up In The Morning .... Triple / Major

Group Dance Activities. Dance activity songs can help develop large gross motor skills, as well as coordination and spatial awareness. Circle dance activities encourage a sense of community and cooperation where everyone moves together. These songs can be sung songs or recordings of classical music. The teacher should choose selections that allow for a circle dance where toddlers can circle right and left and then be spun around, or movement in towards the middle of the circle and back out. The best songs are ones that can be sung while danced, because of the combination of language and movement. These songs can be circle dances or children's games, such as London Bridge, or Ring Around the Rosie, or Did You Ever See A Lassie (where toddlers can swing this way and that).

Classical Instrumental Pieces—do simple circle dances with mom & baby (Circle left/right; move in center lift babies up together; swing side to side; spin around)
.... see Movement Exploration publication and Keeping the Beat CD

Classical Music excerpts: Mozart's Divertimento; Handel's Water Music; etc.
.... see Keeping the Beat CD

Dancing With Teddy (Music Together-Maracas) .... Triple / Major

Everybody Loves Saturday Night (Music Together-Drums) .... Duple / Major

Gallant Ship .... Duple / Major

Goin' To Boston (Music Together-Fiddle) .... Duple / Mixolydian on C

Hey Betty Martin .... Duple / Major

I'm Gonna Play Today (Music Together-Bells) dance / scarves .... Duple / Major

London Bridge .... Duple / Major

Mariá Isabel (Music Together-Triangle) CD#18 .... Duple / Major

Mountain Dew (Music Together-Bongo) CD#16
.... Triple (or Compound Duple) / Major

Noble Duke of York circle dance / drum .... Duple / Major

Palo, Palo (Music Together-Bongo) CD#10 treat like conga line .... Duple / Major

Rig-a-Jig-Jig (Music Together-Drums) .... Triple / Major

Ring Around The Rosie .... Duple / Major

Santa Maloney circle dance / hoops.. Triple / Major

Shake Those 'Simmons Down (Music Together-Flutes) dance & use shakers
.... Duple / Major

Shoo Fly (Music Together-Bongo) CD#17 .... Duple / Major

Skip To My Lou (Music Together-Triangle) CD#7 .... Duple / Major

Focused Listening Activities. These are short examples of sounds of things or animals introduced in songs just sung or songs to come. Listening activities quiet the child and settles the class as well as teaches the child to "actively listen" for something. Listening activities help the child to learn how to focus his/her attention. These activities can help with memory as well as develop auditory acuity. First communicate specifically what to listen for, then the children can then be asked to imitate that sound or even describe it. Of course, imitating the sound is a more desired response than describing it. In this way, listening skills developed. Research connects good listening skills with better grades in school.

    Go to the Internet for animal sounds or sounds focusing on song activities (you can also get ringtones on Google)

Rhythm and Tonal Patterns. Short and simple 2-4 beat rhythmic examples, both duple and triple meter patterns (quarter and eighth note rhythms) and 3-note easy solfége patterns (So-Mi-Do for major, Mi-Do-La for minor) are presented by the teacher and echoed by parents so toddlers can be bathed in rhythmic and tonal patterns taken both from their music and simply created. The teacher chants the neutral syllable "ba" for rhythm patterns, and sings the neutral syllable "bum" for tonal patterns. These patterns can be taken from the rhythm and tonal flash cards in Book 1A of the Knauss Music Curriculum. These patterns can also be taken from the songs just sung, or in the next song to be sung, to help establish tonality (major or minor) or rhythmic meter (duple or triple). These short patterns become the building blocks for children to later identify in music heard or sung, or even to create music of their own. Just like language is learned from words to phrases to sentences, so music is learned the same way; rhythmic and tonal patterns to phrases to creative songs. These patterns help develop a musical vocabulary, which also helps develop memory skills, an important focus skill for K-12 grades and beyond.

    Simple rhythm patterns of quarter and eighth notes on neutral syllable "ba"
    Complex rhythm patterns of any combinations on neutral syllable "ba"
    Duple and Triple rhythm patterns from Book 1A of Knauss Music Curriculum
    Simple tonal patterns of Do-Mi-So using neutral syllable "ba"

Simple tonal patterns of La-Do-Mi using neutral syllable "ba"
Tonal patterns from Book 1A of Knauss Music Curriculum

Hello / Goodbye Songs. Each lesson should contain a "Hello Song" and a "Good-bye Song." These songs may be two different ones, one for Hello and one for Goodbye, or they may be the Hello song with the lyrics changed for Goodbye. These remain the same for the entire class semester. During the hello and goodbye songs, each child's name is sung with a steady beat activity by using a body percussion activity. The Hello song signals the start of class, recognizes the specialness of each child as their name is sung, and allows for repetition (the same song) and variety as well (varying the beat activities). Also sing the names of any guests visiting for the class, such as friends or relatives (aunts, uncles, or grandparents).

Good Morning / What Are You Wearing?	Triple / Major and Duple / Major
Goodbye Now (tune of above Good Morning)	Triple / Major
Goodbye Song (tune of Twinkle, Twinkle)	Duple / Major
Hello Song (Music Together-Bongos) CD #1	Duple / Major
Hello Song (tune of Twinkle, Twinkle)	Duple / Major

Familiar songs with which to change words to Hello or Goodbye:
Clap, Clap, Clap Your Hands
For He's A Jolly Good Fellow
Go Tell Aunt Rhodie
Mary Had A Little Lamb
The More We Get Together
This is The Way We Wash Our Clothes

Toddlers Music Together Books Index

The Music Together Books included in this index are:

Music Together: Tambourine Song Collection
Music Together: Fiddle Song Collection
Music Together: Triangle Song Collection
Music Together: Drum Song Collection
Music Together: Bongos Song Collection
Music Together: Maracas Song Collection
Music Together: Bells Song Collection
Music Together: Sticks Song Collection
Music Together: Flute Song Collection
Music Together: Summer Songs 1
Music Together: Summer Songs 2
Music Together: Summer Songs 3
Music Together: Babies
Music Together: Family Favorites Songbook for Teachers

Music Together: Tambourine Song Collection

Guilmartin, K.K. & Levinowitz, L.M. (2004, 2007). *Music together: Tambourine song collection*. Princeton, NJ: Music Together LLC. www.musictogether.com. (CD, 2007). CD#: MTTA13-CD.

Contents

Betty Martin (Traditional)	p. 19	Duple / Major
Cradle Song (W. Blake & K. Guilmartin)	p. 29	Duple / Major
Ding Dong, Ding Dong (Traditional)	p. 41	Duple / Major / Tonal Round
Good News (Traditional African American Spiritual)	p. 45	Duple / Major
Goodbye, So Long, Farewell (K. Guilmartin)	p. 47	Triple / Major
Green and Blue (K. Guilmartin)	p. 22	Triple Rhythmic Chant
Hello Song (K. Guilmartin)	p. 13	Duple / Major
Hey Ya Na (Traditional Native American Apache)	p. 23	Duple / Natural Minor or Dorian
Hippity, Happity, Hoppity (Doug Morris)	p. 36	Triple Rhythmic Chant
Merry-Go Round (Lynn Lobban)	p. 39	Triple / Minor
Old Brass Wagon (Traditional)	p. 15	Duple / Major

One Little Owl (Traditional)	p. 21	Duple / Minor
Pawpaw Patch (Traditional)	p. 37	Duple / Major
Raisins and Almonds (Traditional)	p. 46	Triple / Minor
Ride-O (Traditional)	p. 16	Duple / Major
Round Robin (Rebecca Frezza)	p. 17	Duple / Major / Tonal Round
Scarborough Fair (Traditional)	p. 43	Triple / Minor
Secrets (K. Guilmartin, L. Levinowitz, & Linda Betlejeski)	p. 40	Duple Rhythmic Chant
See the Pony Galloping (Traditional)	p. 24	Triple / Major
Sneakin' 'Round the Room (K. Guilmartin)	p. 35	Duple / Minor (can be varied or Triple)
Tambourine Jam (K. Guilmartin)	p. 30	Duple / Major / Instrument Play Along with Minor contrasting section
This 'N' That (K. Guilmartin)	p. 42	Duple / Mixolydian (quasi-Cuban)
Tingalayo (Traditional Spanish)	p. 18	Duple / Major
Tricks With Sticks (K. Guilmartin)	p. 26	Duple Rhythmic Chant / Major Tonality in other sections
Wedding Dance (Traditional)	p. 25	Duple / Major with lowered 2nd, 6th, and 7th (Middle Eastern)

Music Together: Fiddle Song Collection

Guilmartin, K.K. & Levinowitz, L.M. (2006, 2009). *Music together: Fiddle song collection*. Princeton, NJ: Music Together LLC. www.musictogether.com. (CD, 2003). CD#: MTFI09-CD.

Contents

A Ram Sam Sam (Traditional)	p. 19	Duple / Major
Apples and Cherries (Traditional)	p. 17	Duple / Major / Tonal Round
Bela Boya (Traditional Bulgarian Folksong)	p. 25	Unusual Meter (7/8) / Implied Dorian Tonality
Butterfly (L. Levinowitz)	p. 40	Triple / Dorian on B
Can You Do This? (K. Guilmartin & L. Levinowitz)	p. 24	Duple / Lydian on C
Crawdad (Traditional)	p. 15	Duple / Major
Goin' To Boston (Traditional American Folksong)	p. 23	Duple / Mixolydian on C
Goodbye, So Long, Farewell (K. Guilmartin)	p. 46	Triple / Major

Hello Song (K. Guilmartin)	p. 13	Duple / Major
Here Is the Beehive (Traditional)	p. 33	Triple Rhythmic Chant
Hiné Ma Tov (Traditional Israeli Folksong)	p. 37	Duple / Dorian on E
I've Got The Rhythm In My Head (American Singing Game)	p. 36	Duple / Major
Lauren's Waltz (K. Guilmartin)	p. 29	Triple / Mixolydian on G (Middle section C Major / Instrumental Play Along)
Los Fandangos (Traditional Spanish Folksong)	p. 22	Triple / Minor
Marching and Drumming (American Civil War Melody)	p. 35	Triple / Natural Minor
Mississippi Cats (K. Guilmartin)	p. 41	Duple Rhythmic Chant
No More Pie (Traditional)	p. 39	Duple / Minor Blues
Old King Cole (K. Guilmartin)	p. 21	Duple / Natural Minor
Shady Grove (Traditional)	p. 28	Duple / Re Pentatonic based on C
Shenandoah (Traditional American Folksong)	p. 45	Duple / Major
Singin' Every Day (K. Guilmartin, South African Melody)	p. 43	Duple / Major
Sweet Potato (Traditional Afro-American Folksong)	p. 27	Duple / Major
The Sounds Of Fall (K. Guilmartin)	p. 16	Duple Rhythmic Chant
This Little Light Of Mine (Traditional)	p. 44	Duple / Major
Walking Song (K. Guilmartin)	p. 18	Duple / Mixolydian on D

Music Together: Triangle Song Collection

Guilmartin, K.K. & Levinowitz, L.M. (2003, 2006). *Music together: Triangle song collection*. Princeton, NJ: Music Together LLC. www.musictogether.com. (CD, 2006). CD#: MTTR12-CD.

Contents

Allee Galloo (Traditional)	p. 45	Triple / Major
Ally Bally (Traditional)	p. 29	Duple / Major
Baa, Baa, Little Star (K. Guilmartin)	p. 30	Duple / Major / Instrumental Play Along
Bird Song (Doug Morris)	p. 39	Triple / Phrygian on C
Breezes (K. Guilmartin)	p. 35	Triple / Mixolydian on D
Camels (K. Guilmartin)	p. 25	Duple / Implied Major with lowered 2nd
Can You Do What I Do? (Traditional)	p. 21	Duple Rhythmic Chant
Dance with Me (Traditional)	p. 14	Duple & Triple / Major
Drummers Marching (Linda Jessup)	p. 42	Triple / Minor

Goodbye, So Long, Farewell (K. Guilmartin)	p. 47	Triple / Major
Hello Song (K. Guilmartin)	p. 13	Duple / Major
Hey, Ho, Nobody Home (Traditional)	p. 28	Duple (Swing Rhythm) / Minor
I'm Hiding (K. Guilmartin)	p. 37	Duple Rhythmic Chant
Ladybug (Lynn Lobban)	p. 19	Triple / Dorian Implied
Mariá Isabel (Traditional Spanish Folksong)	p. 27	Duple / Major
Nothin' Blues (K. Guilmartin & J.C. Lewis)	p. 18	Duple / Major in Blues Style
Old Blue (Traditional)	p. 38	Duple / Mixolydian on D
Rain Song (K. Guilmartin)	p. 20	Duple / Dorian on D
Rolling a Round Ball (Sally Weaver)	p. 24	Triple / Dorian on C
Skip to My Lou (Traditional)	p. 41	Duple / Major
Stick Dance (K. Guilmartin)	p. 43	Unusual Meter (5/4) / Various Implied Tonalities (Lydian) and some Blues
Ten Fingers (Traditional)	p. 17	Duple Rhythmic Chant
The Train Song (Art Levinowitz)	p. 15	Duple / Major (Vocal Harmony Parts)
The Water is Wide (Traditional)	p. 46	Duple / Major
Two Little Blackbirds (K. Guilmartin)	p. 23	Duple / Major

Music Together: Drum Song Collection

Guilmartin, K.K. & Levinowitz, L.M. (2007, 2010). *Music together: Drum song collection*. Princeton, NJ: Music Together LLC. www.musictogether.com. (CD, 2012). CD#: MTDR13-CD.

Contents

Arirang (Traditional Korean Folksong)	p. 44	Triple / Do Pentatonic on G with accidental Bb)
Biddy Biddy (Traditional)	p. 14	Duple / Major
Clap Your Hands (Traditional)	p. 15	Duple / Mixolydian on D
Drum and Sing (K. Guilmartin)	p. 41	Duple / Minor
Duérmete Niño Bonito (Traditional Spanish Folksong)	p. 29	Triple / Minor
Everybody Loves Saturday Night (Traditional)	p. 45	Duple / Major
Goodbye, So Long, Farewell (K. Guilmartin)	p. 47	Triple / Major
Hello Song (K. Guilmartin)	p. 13	Duple / Major
John the Rabbit (Traditional)	p. 17	Duple / Major
Kookaburra (Traditional)	p. 43	Duple / Major
My Ball (L. Levinowitz)	p. 25	Unusual Meter (7/8) Rhythmic Chant

Play Along (K. Guilmartin)	p. 30	Duple / Major / Instrumental Play Along
Playin' in the Kitchen (K. Guilmartin)	p. 39	Duple Rhythmic Chant and Major Tonal Singing
Pussycat (J. Kuhns)	p. 23	Mixed Triple / Phrygian on E
Rig-A-Jig-Jig (Traditional)	p. 40	Triple / Major
Roll Over (Traditional)	p. 21	Duple / Major
Sailing Song (L. Levinowitz)	p. 26	Triple / Mixolydian on D
She Sells Sea Shells (K. Guilmartin)	p. 19	Duple / Implied Dorian on D
Sneak and Peak (L. Levinowitz)	p. 20	Duple / Dorian on D
The Snail and the Mouse (Traditional)	p. 18	Duple Rhythmic Chant
There's a Cobbler (Traditional)	p. 33	Duple Rhythmic Chant
They Come Back (K. Guilmartin)	p. 35	Duple / Major
This Train (Traditional)	p. 27	Duple / Dorian on D Countermelodies)
Ticking and Tocking (K. Guilmartin & L. Levinowitz)	p. 24	Triple / Lydian on F
Tomorrow's Now Today (K. Guilmartin & L. Guilmartin)	p. 46	Duple / Major

Music Together: Bongos Song Collection

Guilmartin, K.K. & Levinowitz, L.M. (2008). *Music together: Bongos song collection*. Princeton, NJ: Music Together LLC. www.musictogether.com. (CD, 2005). CD#: MTBO11-CD.

Contents

Bongo Jam (K. Guilmartin)	p. 28	Duple / Major / Instrumental Play Along
Canoe Song (Traditional)	p. 39	Duple / Minor
City Blues (K. Guilmartin)	p. 45	Duple / Major
Ding-A-Ding (K. Guilmartin)	p. 24	Duple / Dorian / Combinable
Down Under (K. Guilmartin)	p. 43	Unusual Paired (6/8 & 4/4)
Eensy, Weensy Spider (Traditional American)	p. 33	Triple (or Compound Duple) / Major
Every Day (K. Guilmartin)	p. 15	Combined (Duple with Triplets) / Rhythm Activity
Fireworks (L. Levinowitz)	p. 22	Triple / Rhythm Round
Goodbye, So Long, Farewell (K. Guilmartin)	p. 47	Triple / Major
Greensleeves (Traditional English)	p. 36	Triple / Harmonic Minor

Hello Song (K. Guilmartin) .... p. 13	Duple / Major
Hey, Diddle, Diddle (K. Guilmartin)........................... p. 17	Duple / Minor
Li'L 'Liza Jane / Funga Alafia (Traditional Afro-American) .... p. 40	Duple / Major / Partner Songs
Little Johnny Brown (Traditional Afro-American)..... p. 37	Duple / Natural Minor
Mountain Dew (Traditional Irish) .... p. 34	Triple (or Compound Duple) / Major
My Bonnie (H. J. Fulmer) .... p. 46	Triple / Major
Open and Shut Them (Traditional Flemish).............. p. 16	Duple / Major
Palo, Palo (Traditional Dominican Republic) .... p. 23	Duple / Major
See How I'm Jumping (Traditional Flemish) .... p. 20	Duple / Minor
She'll Be Comin' 'Round the Mountain (Traditional American) .... p. 14	Duple / Major
Shoo, Fly, Don't Bother Me (Frank Campbell & Billy Reeves) .... p. 35	Duple / Major
Sleepyhead (Lyn Ransom).. p. 27	Duple / Major
This Old Man (Traditional)....................................... p. 21	Duple / Major
Train is a-Comin' (Traditional Afro-American).......... p. 25	Duple / Major
Walking Through the Woods (K. Guilmartin)........... p. 19	Triple / Minor

Music Together: Maracas Song Collection

Guilmartin, K.K. & Levinowitz, L.M. (2005, 2008). *Music together: Maracas song collection*. Princeton, NJ: Music Together LLC. www.musictogether.com.

Contents

All Around The Kitchen (Traditional) .... p. 18	Duple / Three classic blues forms of 12-bar, 8-bar, & 16-bar on A Minor
Bim Bam (Traditional)... p. 22	Duple / Minor
Brincan Y Bailan (Traditional) .... p. 36	Duple / Minor
Cloud Song (Linda Jessup)....................................... p. 41	Triple / Minor
Dancing With Teddy (K. Guilmartin) .... p. 35	Triple / Major
Dee Da Dum (K. Guilmartin) .... p. 37	Duple / Major / Jazz Style
Doodle (L. Levinowitz) .... p. 27	Duple (Swing) / Dorian on D
Five Little Mice (Traditional).................................... p. 33	Duple Rhythmic Chant
Frère Jacques (Traditional) .... p. 44	Duple / Major / Vocal and Instrumental Ostinatos
Goin' For Coffee (K. Guilmartin) .... p. 30	Duple / Blues on C / Instrumental Play Along
Goodbye, So Long, Farwell (K. Guilmartin).............. p. 46	Triple / Major
Hello Song (K. Guilmartin) .... p. 13	Duple / Major

Bitty Bops—Toddlers—Document 15

Song	Page	Meter/Tonality
Hop Ol' Squirrel (Traditional)	p. 25	Duple / Major
I'm A Bell (L. Levinowitz)	p. 23	Triple / Minor
Jack Be Nimble (K. Guilmartin)	p. 40	Triple Rhythmic Chant
Jumpin' Josie (Traditional)	p. 14	Duple / Do Pentatonic on D
Pease Porridge Hot (Traditional)	p. 15	Duple Rhythmic Chant
Play the Drum (K. Guilmartin)	p. 43	Duple / Major
Russian Folk Song (Traditional)	p. 45	Duple / Major
Su La Li (Bonnie Light)	p. 29	Duple / Minor
The Sad Little Puppy (K. Guilmartin)	p. 39	Duple / Minor
Train To the City (Traditional)	p. 28	Duple / Major
Tsakonikos (Traditional)	p. 26	Unusual Meter (5/4) / Natural Minor
Wiggle! (L. Levinowitz)	p. 17	Duple / Major
William Tell's Ride (Rossini, arr. L. Ransom & K. Guilmartin)	p. 21	Duple / Major and Minor

Music Together: Bells Song Collection

Guilmartin, K.K. & Levinowitz, L.M. (2009). *Music together: Bells song collection*. Princeton, NJ: Music Together LLC. www.musictogether.com.

Contents

Song	Page	Meter/Tonality
Brahms' Lullaby (Johannes Brahms)	p. 44	Triple / Major
By 'n' By (Traditional)	p. 29	Duple / Major
Celebration Song (Traditional Hasidic)	p. 23	Duple / Israeli Scale (Major with lowered 2nd)
De Colores (Traditional Mexican)	p. 27	Triple / Major
Deedle Dumpling (Chris Posluszny)	p. 25	Duple / Dorian
Foolin' Around (K. Guilmartin)	p. 30	Duple / Minor & Major / Instrumental
French Folk Song (Traditional French)	p. 37	Duple / Major
French Folk Song [Teacher Mixes] (on CD)		
Goodbye, So Long, Farewell (K. Guilmartin)	p. 45	Triple / Major
Hello Song (K. Guilmartin)	p. 13	Duple / Major
Hopping and Sliding (K. Guilmartin)	p. 18	Usual Paired (2/4 & 3/4) / Minor & Major
I'm Gonna Play Today (Traditional American)	p. 14	Duple / Major
Lukey's Boat (Traditional)	p. 26	Duple / Major
Me, You, and We (K. Guilmartin)	p. 36	Duple / Major
Misty Morning (K. Guilmartin)	p. 39	Triple / Minor (D Dorian & Natural)
Mr. Rabbit (Traditional)	p. 43	Duple / Major
My Lady Wind (K. Guilmartin)	p. 19	Duple / Major

Song	Page	Style
Obwisana (Traditional Ghana)	p. 21	Duple / Major
Rhythms and Rhymes [Teacher Mixes] (on CD)		
Rhythms and Rhymes	p. 15	Duple Rhythm Chant
Robby Roly (K. Guilmartin)	p. 38	Duple / Minor
Robby Roly [Teacher Mixes] (on CD)		
Snowflakes (L. Levinowitz)	p. 22	Unusual (5/8) / Rhythmic Chant
Splishing and Splashing (K. Guilmartin)	p. 35	Duple with Triplets / Rhythmic Chant
The Bells of Westminster (Traditional)	p. 42	Duple / Major / Round & Countermelodies
The Bells of Westminster [Teacher Mixes] (on CD)		
Trot, Old Joe (Traditional)	p. 41	Duple / Major
Two Little Kitty Cats (Traditional)	p. 17	Duple / Minor
Who's That? (Traditional)	p. 33	Duple / Major

Music Together: Sticks Song Collection

Guilmartin, K.K. & Levinowitz, L.M. (2010). *Music together: Sticks song collection*. Princeton, NJ: Music Together LLC. www.musictogether.com. (CD, 2007). CD#: MTST11-CD.

Contents

Song	Page	Style
Blow the Wind Southerly (Traditional)	p. 37	Triple / Major
Don Alfredo Baila (Traditional Catalonian)	p. 39	Duple / Major
Follow Me Down to Carlow (Traditional)	p. 17	Triple / Minor (or Dorian)
Goodbye, So Long, Farewell (K. Guilmartin)	p. 45	Triple / Major
Great Big Stars (Traditional Appalachian)		Duple / Major
Happy Puppy, Silly Cat (Sally Weaver)	p. 22	Unusual (7/8) / Major
Hello Song (K. Guilmartin)	p. 13	Duple / Major
Husha My Baby (Traditional South African)		Duple / Minor
I'm Freezing! (K. Guilmartin)	p. 24	Duple Chant
Jack-In-The-Box (Traditional)	p. 35	Triple / Rhythm Chant
Mary Wore a Red Dress (Traditional)	p. 18	Duple / Major
May All Children (K. Guilmartin)	p. 44	Multi-Metric (2/4, 3/4, 4/4) / Major
Mix It Up! (K. Guilmartin)	p. 38	Duple / G Mixolydian
Nigun (Traditional)	p. 25	Duple / Minor
Play Along, Too (K. Guilmartin)	p. 31	Duple / Major / Instrumental
Pop! Goes the Weasel (Traditional)	p. 28	Compound Triple (6/8) / Major
Ridin' in the Car (K. Guilmartin)	p. 15	Duple / Major

Roll That Little Ball (Traditional)	p. 27	Duple / Major
Spin and Stop (L. Levinowitz)	p. 19	Triple Minor
Stick Tune (K. Guilmartin)	p. 21	Duple / D Mixolydian
The Love Song of Kangding (Traditional Sichuan Chinese)		Duple / Minor
The Tailor and the Mouse (Traditional)	p. 36	Duple / Minor
Trot to Grandma's House (Traditional)	p. 41	Duple / Major
Water Play (K. Guilmartin)		Triple Rhythm Activity
When the Saints Go Marching In (Traditional)	p. 43	Duple / Major

Music Together: Flute Song Collection

Guilmartin, K.K. & Levinowitz, L.M. (2010). *Music together: Flute song collection.* Princeton, NJ: Music Together LLC. www.musictogether.com.

Contents

Aeolian Dance (K. Guilmartin)	p. 21	Duple / Aeolian / Sung Neutral Syllable & Danced
All the Pretty Little Horses (Traditional)	p. 45	Duple / Minor (Aeolian or Natural)
Dance to Your Daddy (Traditional)	p. 35	Triple / Minor
Dum Ditty Dum (Traditional)	p. 18	Duple / Major
Goodbye, So Long, Farewell (K. Guilmartin)	p. 46	Triple / Major
Harvest Dance (K. Guilmartin & L. Levinowitz)	p. 40	Triple / Major / Sung Neutral Syllable & Danced
Hello Song (K. Guilmartin)	p. 13	Duple / Major
Hey Lolly, Lolly (Traditional)	p. 14	Duple / Major
I Had a Little Frog (Traditional)	p. 15	Duple Rhythm Chant
I've Been Working on the Railroad (Traditional)	p. 43	Duple / Major
Jim Along Josie (Traditional)	p. 33	Duple / Major
Leaves Are Falling (Rebecca Frezza)	p. 27	Duple / Dorian on E / Round
Ran Tin Tinnah (Traditional Celtic)	p. 25	Duple / Major
Rocketship (Rebecca Frezza)	p. 36	Unusual (5/4) / Rhythmic Chant
Sandpiper (K. Guilmartin)	p. 20	Duple / Major
Saying and Doing (K. Guilmartin)	p. 23	Triple Rhythmic Chant
Shake Those 'Simmons Down (Traditional)	p. 28	Duple / Major
Simple Gifts (Traditional)	p. 30	Duple / Major / Instrumental Play Along
The Crow Song (Traditional)	p. 37	Duple / Major / Sung Neutral Syllable
The Earth is Our Mother (Traditional)	p. 19	Duple / Minor
The Riddle Song (Traditional)	p. 29	Duple / Major
The Three Ravens (Traditional)	p. 17	Duple / Minor
There's a Little Wheel a-Turnin' (Traditional)	p. 24	Duple / Major
Tum Balalaika (Traditional)	p. 41	Triple / Minor
Vengan a Ver (Traditional Argentinian)	p. 39	Duple / Major

Music Together: Summer Songs 1

Guilmartin, K.K. & Levinowitz, L.M. (2001). *Music together: Summer songs 1*. Princeton, NJ: Music Together LLC. www.musictogether.com.

Contents

A Ram Sam Sam (Traditional)	p. 20	Duple / Major
Deedle Dumpling (Chris Posluszny)	p. 33	Duple / Dorian
Goodbye, So Long, Farewell (K. Guilmartin)	p. 39	Triple / Major
Happy Puppy, Silly Cat (Sally Weaver)	p. 27	Unusual (7/8) / Major
Hello Song (K. Guilmartin)	p. 11	Duple / Major
Here Is the Beehive (Traditional)	p. 13	Triple Rhythmic Chant
Hey, Diddle, Diddle (K. Guilmartin)	p. 12	Duple / Minor
Hiné Ma Tov (Traditional Israeli Folksong)	p. 16	Duple / Dorian on E
I've Got The Rhythm In My Head (American Singing Game)	p. 17	Duple / Major
Jim Along Josie (Traditional)	p. 35	Duple / Major
Mariá Isabel (Traditional Spanish Folksong)	p. 37	Duple / Major
My Bonnie (H. J. Fulmer)	p. 38	Triple / Major
My Lady Wind (K. Guilmartin)	p. 21	Duple / Major
Play Along (K. Guilmartin)	p. 25	Duple / Major / Instrumental Play Along
Play the Drum (K. Guilmartin)	p. 15	Duple / Major
Rolling a Round Ball (Sally Weaver)	p. 30	Triple / Dorian on C
Ten Fingers (Traditional)	p. 19	Duple Rhythmic Chant
The Two Birds (Mother Goose)	p. 31	Duple Rhythm Chant with Triplets
Tomorrow's Now Today (K. Guilmartin & L. Guilmartin)	p. 24	Duple / Major
Tricks With Sticks (K. Guilmartin)	p. 22	Duple Rhythmic Chant / Major Tonality in other sections
Two Little Kitty Cats (Traditional)	p. 29	Duple / Minor

Music Together: Summer Songs 2

Guilmartin, K.K. & Levinowitz, L.M. (2007). *Music together: Summer songs 2*. Princeton, NJ: Music Together LLC. www.musictogether.com.

Contents

Song	Page	Tonality
Allee Galloo (Traditional)	p. 37	Triple / Major
Butterfly (L. Levinowitz)	p. 36	Triple / Dorian on B
Crawdad (Traditional)	p. 15	Duple / Major
Doodle (L. Levinowitz)	p. 33	Duple (Swing) / Dorian on D
Eensy, Weensy Spider (Traditional American)	p. 18	Triple (or Compound Duple) / Major
Fireworks (L. Levinowitz)	p. 19	Triple Rhythmic Chant
Five Little Mice (Traditional)	p. 16	Duple Rhythmic Chant
Foolin' Around (K. Guilmartin)	p. 28	Duple / Minor & Major / Instrumental
Goodbye, So Long, Farewell (K. Guilmartin)	p. 40	Triple / Major
Hello Song (K. Guilmartin)	p. 13	Duple / Major
Here Is the Beehive (Traditional)	p. 31	Triple Rhythmic Chant
John the Rabbit (Traditional)	p. 25	Duple / Major
Mariá Isabel (Traditional Spanish Folksong)	p. 35	Duple / Major
Ridin' in the Car (K. Guilmartin)	p. 22	Duple / Major
She Sells Sea Shells (K. Guilmartin)	p. 23	Duple / Implied Dorian on D
Sleepyhead (Lyn Ransom)	p. 39	Duple / Major
Stick Dance (K. Guilmartin)	p. 26	Unusual Meter (5/4) / Various Implied Tonalities (Lydian) and some Blues
Su La Li (Bonnie Light)	p. 27	Duple / Minor
The Sad Little Puppy (K. Guilmartin)	p. 21	Duple / Minor
The Train Song (Art Levinowitz)	p. 17	Duple / Major (Vocal Harmony Parts)
Trot, Old Joe (Traditional)	p. 32	Duple / Major

Music Together: Summer Songs 3

Guilmartin, K.K. & Levinowitz, L.M. (2002). *Music together: Summer songs 3*. Princeton, NJ: Music Together LLC. www.musictogether.com.

Contents

Song	Page	Style
All the Pretty Little Horses (Traditional)	p. 27	Duple / Minor (Aeolian or Natural)
Apples and Cherries (Traditional)	p. 23	Duple / Major / Tonal Round
Baa, Baa, Little Star (K. Guilmartin)	p. 28	Duple / Major / Instrumental Play Along
Goodbye, So Long, Farewell (K. Guilmartin)	p. 42	Triple / Major
Hello Song (K. Guilmartin)	p. 13	Duple / Major
Here is a Bunny (Traditional)	p. 33	Triple Rhythm Chant
Hey, Ho, Nobody Home (Traditional)	p. 26	Duple (Swing Rhythm) / Minor
I Had a Little Frog (Traditional)	p. 14	Duple Rhythm Chant
Marching and Drumming (American Civil War Melody)	p. 18	Triple / Natural Minor
Me, You, and We (K. Guilmartin)	p. 15	Duple / Major
My Ball (L. Levinowitz)	p. 25	Unusual Meter (7/8) Rhythmic Chant
Obwisana (Traditional Ghana)	p. 17	Duple / Major
Old King Cole (K. Guilmartin)	p. 35	Duple / Natural Minor
Pussycat (J. Kuhns)	p. 21	Mixed Triple / Phrygian on E
Russian Folk Song (Traditional)	p. 41	Duple / Major
Sailing Song (L. Levinowitz)	p. 19	Triple / Mixolydian on D
See the Pony Galloping (Traditional)	p. 22	Triple / Major
Shake Those 'Simmons Down (Traditional)	p. 40	Duple / Major
Singin' Every Day (K. Guilmartin, South African Melody)	p. 39	Duple / Major
There's a Little Wheel a-Turnin' (Traditional)	p. 36	Duple / Major
Tingalayo (Traditional Spanish)	p. 37	Duple / Major

Music Together: Babies

Guilmartin, K.K. & Levinowitz, L.M. (2002). *Music together: Babies*. Princeton, NJ: Music Together LLC. www.musictogether.com.

Contents

All the Pretty Little Horses (Traditional)	p. 33	Duple / Minor (Aeolian or Natural)
Allee Galloo (Traditional)	p. 39	Triple / Major
Bela Boya (Traditional Bulgarian Folksong)	p. 30	Unusual Meter (7/8) / Implied Dorian Tonality
Breezes (K. Guilmartin)	p. 27	Triple / Mixolydian on D
Dee Da Dum (K. Guilmartin)	p. 23	Duple / Major / Jazz Style
Eensy, Weensy Spider (Traditional American)	p. 25	Triple (or Compound Duple) / Major
Every Day (K. Guilmartin)	p. 22	Combined (Duple with Triplets) / Rhythm Activity
Fireworks (L. Levinowitz)	p. 26	Triple Rhythmic Chant
Goodbye, So Long, Farewell (K. Guilmartin)	p. 52	Triple / Major
Hello Song (K. Guilmartin)	p. 19	Duple / Major
Here Is the Beehive (Traditional)	p. 41	Triple Rhythmic Chant
Hey Ya Na (Traditional Native American—Apache)	p. 45	Duple / Natural Minor
Mary Wore a Red Dress (Traditional)	p. 50	Duple / Major
Merry-Go Round (Lynn Lobban)	p. 40	Triple / Minor
My Bonnie (H. J. Fulmer)	p. 51	Triple / Major
Obwisana (Traditional Ghana)	p. 43	Duple / Major
Simple Gifts (Traditional)	p. 34	Duple / Major / Instrumental Play Along
Sneakin' 'Round the Room (K. Guilmartin)	p. 49	Duple / Minor (can be varied for Triple)
Sweet Potato (Traditional Afro-American Folksong)	p. 29	Duple / Major
There's a Little Wheel a-Turnin' (Traditional)	p. 31	Duple / Major
Tingalayo (Traditional Spanish)	p. 32	Duple / Major
To Market (Traditional & K. Guilmartin)	p. 44	Triple Rhythm Chant
Trot to Grandma's House (Traditional)	p. 21	Duple / Major
Who's That? (Traditional)	p. 37	Duple / Major
William Tell's Ride (Rossini, arr. L. Ransom & K. Guilmartin)	p. 47	Duple / Major and Minor

Music Together: Family Favorites Songbook for Teachers

Guilmartin, K.K. & Levinowitz, L.M. (2009). *Music together: Family favorites songbook for teachers: Bringing harmony home*. Princeton, NJ: Music Together LLC. www.musictogether.com. ISBN: 978-0-615-32865-2.

Contents

Song	Page	Style
Allee Galloo (Traditional)	p. 88	Triple / Major
Biddy Biddy (Traditional)	p. 26	Duple / Major
Dancing With Teddy (K. Guilmartin)	p. 84	Triple / Major
Goin' For Coffee (K. Guilmartin)	p. 70	Duple / Blues on C / Instrumental Play Along
Goodbye, So Long, Farewell (K. Guilmartin)	p. 96	Triple / Major
Hello Song (K. Guilmartin)	p. 22	Duple / Major
I've Been Working on the Railroad (Traditional)	p. 80	Duple / Major
John the Rabbit (Traditional)	p. 54	Duple / Major
May All Children (K. Guilmartin)	p. 92	Multi-Metric (2/4, 3/4, 4/4) / Major
Mississippi Cats (K. Guilmartin)	p. 62	Duple Rhythmic Chant
Obwisana (Traditional Ghana)	p. 76	Duple / Major
One Little Owl (Traditional)	p. 66	Duple / Minor
Palo, Palo (Traditional Dominican Republic)	p. 50	Duple / Major
Playin' in the Kitchen (K. Guilmartin)	p. 46	Duple Rhythmic Chant and Major Tonal Singing
Ridin' in the Car (K. Guilmartin)	p. 34	Duple / Major
She Sells Sea Shells (K. Guilmartin)	p. 42	Duple / Implied Dorian on D
Spin and Stop (L. Levinowitz)	p. 58	Triple Minor
Splishing and Splashing (K. Guilmartin)	p. 30	Duple with Triplets / Rhythmic Chant
Stick Tune (K. Guilmartin)	p. 38	Duple / D Mixolydian

Toddlers Music Play Index

Music Play: Book 1

Valerio, W., Reynolds, A., Bolton, B., Taggart, C., & Gordon, E. (2000). *Music play: Book 1: The early childhood music curriculum guide for parents, teachers and caregivers*. Chicago, IL: GIA Publications, Inc. Item #G-J236. ISBN: 1-57999-027-4.

The *Music Play* guide includes 57 songs and rhythm chants in a variety of tonalities and meters and over 200 music and movement activities designed to assist you in organizing sequential music and movement experiences for newborn and young children. Each of the songs and rhythm chants found in the guide is recorded on the accompanying compact disc or cassette.

Valerio, W., Reynolds, A., Bolton, B., Taggart, C., & Gordon, E. (1998). *Music play: CD: The early childhood music curriculum guide for parents, teachers and caregivers*. Chicago, IL: GIA Publications, Inc. Item #CD-426.

The beautiful full-color book and CD set includes photos of children engaged in music activities. The book includes notation and lesson plans adapted to the individual needs of each child, as well as a complete introduction to how young children learn when they learn music.

Contents

Songs Without Words (sing with tonal neutral syllable "bum") .... pp. 49-76

"Ring the Bells" .... p. 50 — Major / Duple
- Acculturation Tonal Pattern 1 — Major
- Imitation Tonal Pattern 1 — Major
- Imitation Tonal Pattern 2 — Major
- Assimilation Pattern Activities

"My Mommy is a Pilot" .... p. 52 — Major / Duple
- Acculturation Tonal Pattern 1 — Major
- Imitation Tonal Pattern 1 — Major
- Imitation Tonal Pattern 2 — Major
- Assimilation Pattern Activities

"Bumble Bee" .... p. 54 — Major / Multi-Metric (Unusual Paired 5/8 & Triple)
- Acculturation Tonal Pattern 1 — Major
- Imitation Tonal Pattern 1 — Major
- Imitation Tonal Pattern 2 — Major
- Assimilation Pattern Activities

Song	Page	Tonality / Meter
"I Saw a Dinosaur"	p. 56	Major / Duple

(Acculturation, Imitation, Assimilation activities continue with each song)

Song	Page	Tonality / Meter
"Winter Day"	p. 58	Harmonic Minor / Unusual Paired (5/8)
"The Sled"	p. 60	Harmonic Minor / Triple / ABA Form
"Pennsylvania Dreamin'"	p. 62	Harmonic Minor / Triple
"Planting Flowers"	p. 64	Melodic Minor / Triple
"Goldfish"	p. 66	Dorian / Triple
"Dancing"	p. 67	Dorian / Duple
"Jumping"	p. 68	Dorian" / Triple
"Ocean Waves"	p. 69	Dorian / Triple
"Country Dance"	p. 70	Mixolydian / Triple
"Red Umbrella"	p. 71	Dorian / Unusual Unpaired (7/8) / Ritardando
"Albany"	p. 72	Mixolydian / Multi-Metric (Triple & Duple)
"Good-bye"	p. 73	Phrygian / Triple
"Stirring Soup"	p. 74	Phrygian / Unusual Paired (5/8)
"Daydreams"	p. 75	Locrian / Duple

Chants Without Words (chant with rhythm neutral syllable "ba") ....pp. 77-98

"Follow Me!"	p. 78	Duple
"Stretch and Bounce"	p. 80	Duple
"Walking With My Mom"	p. 82	Duple / Accent
"Fireworks"	p. 84	Duple / Crescendo / Subito
"Rolling"	p. 86	Triple
"Popsicle"	p. 88	Triple / Crescendo / Decrescendo / Same and Different
"Child Song"	p. 90	Triple
"Snowflake"	p. 92	Harmonic Minor (Recorded accompaniment) / Triple
"Rain"	p. 94	Unusual Paired (5/8) / Timbre Awareness
"Panda"	p. 95	Unusual Paired (5/8)
"Buggy Ride"	p. 96	Unusual Unpaired (7/8) / Accent
"Wild Pony"	p. 97	Unusual Unpaired (7/8) / Accent
"Train Ride"	p. 98	Unusual Unpaired (7/8) / Accent

Songs With Words .... pp. 99-111

    "Down By the Station"................................p. 100   Major / Duple
    "Jeremiah Blow the Fire"............................p. 101   Major / Duple
    "Roll the Ball Like This"..............................p. 102   Harmonic Minor / Triple
    "My Pony Bill"..p. 103   Harmonic Minor / Triple
    "Ni, Nah, Noh"..p. 104   Aeolian / Triple / Ritardando / Same and Different

    "Bushes and Briars".....................................p. 105   Dorian / Triple / Same and Different

    "To the Window"...p. 106   Dorian or Aeolian / Unusual Paired (5/8)

    "Swinging" ....p. 107   Mixolydian / Triple
    "Jerry Hall"..p. 108   Mixolydian / Unusual Paired (5/8)

    "The Wind" ....p. 109   Lydian / Triple
    "Poor Bengy" ....p. 110   Phrygian / Duple
    "North and South".....................................p. 111   Locrian / Duple

Chants With Words .... pp. 112-124

    "My Mother, Your Mother"........................p. 113   Duple
    "Popcorn" ....p. 114   Duple
    "Go and Stop"...p. 115   Duple
    "Sidewalk Talk"...p. 116   Duple
    "This Little Piggy ....p. 117   Triple
    "Clackety Clack"..p. 118   Triple
    "Hickety Pickety Bumble Bee".....................p. 119   Triple
    "Here is the Beehive" ....p. 120   Triple / Tempo (Quick and Slow)

    "Jump Over the Ocean" ....p. 121   Triple
    "Flop"..p. 122   Unusual Unpaired (7/8)
    "In the Tub" ....p. 123   Unusual Unpaired (7/8)
    "Hop and Stop"...p. 124   Multi-Metric (Unusual Paired 5/8 & Triple)

Toddlers Nichol's Worth Books Index

A Nichol's Worth
Volumes 1, 2, 3, & 4

Nichol, Doug (1975). *A Nichol's worth. Volumes 1 & 2 (1975). Volumes 3 & 4 (1978).* Buffalo, NY: Tometic Associates LTD. Reprinted with permission. University Park, PA: The Pennsylvania State University Bookstore.

A collection of witty, folk-like songs in four volumes, featuring duple, triple, and multi-metric combined meters; in Major, Minor, Dorian, Mixolydian, Phrygian, Lydian, and multi-tonal modes; and in vocal textures of unison, combinable songs, partner songs, ostinatos, countermelodies, and rounds.

Contents

A Nichol's Worth, Volume I .... pp. 1-52

"Acceptance"	p. 42	Combined Meter (Duple with Triplets) / Minor / Unison
"Boy I'm Gonna Get Stuffed With Food"	p. 12	Triple / Dorian / Unison
"Changeable Chug-a-lug"	p. 50	Duple / Triple / Major / Combinable
"Do You Believe It?"	p. 26	Duple / Major / Partner
"Fireman, Fireman"	p. 5	Duple / Minor / Ostinato
"Freedom"	p. 32	Duple / Major / Countermelody
"Grandma Has a Habit"	p. 2	Triple / Mixolydian / Countermelody
"The Grasshopper and the Elephant"	p. 9	Duple / Phrygian / Unison
"Happiness is Giving"	p. 15	Duple / Mixolydian / Partner
"Hot Dog"	p. 4	Unusual Meter (5/8) / Major / Unison
"I Don't Believe It"	p. 27	Duple / Major / Partner
"I'm Your Friend"	p. 14	Duple / Mixolydian / Partner
"I Want to Be Lonely"	p. 22	Duple / Major / Unison
"I Would Give You the World"	p. 36	Triple / Major / Unison
"Let's Make It Christmas All the Time"	p. 16	Duple / Major / Countermelodies
"Look For the Bright Side"	p. 38	Duple / Major / Combinable
"Love Would Increase"	p. 44	Duple / Dorian / Countermelodies
"New Shoes"	p. 6	Duple / Major / Unison

Song	Page	Description
"Nobody Cares"	p. 40	Duple / Lydian / Countermelodies
"One of These Days"	p. 35	Unusual (6/8 with Duple & Triple) / Mixolydian / Round
"Peas"	p. 1	Triple / Lydian / Unison
"The Secret"	p. 30	Duple / Minor / Unison
"The Squirrel"	p. 8	Triple / Phrygian / Unison
"There Won't Be Any to Save"	p. 24	Duple / Major / Unison
"Time"	p. 46	Duple / Major / Countermelody
"What Am I?"	p. 28	Duple / Mixolydian / Ostinato
"When I'm Thinking of You"	p. 19	Duple / Major / Combinable
"Where In the World Did I Put My Mittens?"	p. 10	Duple / Major / Unison
"Who Says?"	p. 20	Duple / Mixolydian / Unison

A Nichol's Worth, Volume II .... pp. 1-52

Song	Page	Description
"Autumn"	p. 22	Triple / Minor & Dorian / Countermelody
"Bangity Wangity Wapsy Boom"	p. 1	Triple / Major / Unison
"Boy, I Wish I Were Ninety Feet Tall"	p. 2	Triple / Dorian / Unison
"Come On You People"	p. 51	Duple / Major / Round
"Chug-a-lug Choo Choo"	p. 29	Unusual (5/8) / Major / Round
"The Eagle"	p. 50	Duple / Minor / Unison
"Eletelephony"	p. 3	Duple / Mixolydian / Unison
"Funny Shape"	p. 20	Triple / Lydian / Countermelodies
"Give a Little Love"	p. 30	Duple / Major / Combinable
"H-A-double P-I-N-E-double S"	p. 8	Duple / Major / Unison
"The Hootchy Kootchy Dance"	p. 6	Duple / Mixolydian / Countermelodies
"I Do Better When I Try My Best"	p. 40	Duple / Major / Countermelody
"I'm Tired of Bein' Busy"	p. 42	Duple / Major / Unison
"It's Not Too Bad to Be Me"	p. 46	Duple / Lydian / Combinable
"Living Spring"	p. 10	Combined (Duple with Triplets) / Major / Round
"Oh, It's Great to Be Living This Morning"	p. 34	Duple / Major / Combinable
"The Old Swamp Band"	p. 26	Duple / Major / Unison
"Over"	p. 39	Duple / Major / Unison
"People Who Need Your Help"	p. 16	Duple / Major / Countermelodies
"Sam, Sam, the Butcher Man"	p. 9	Duple / Lydian / Ostinatos
"Snow"	p. 44	Triple / Major / Combinable

"Summer Is"	p. 11	Triple / Mixolydian / Round
"The Summer's Near"	p. 48	Duple / Minor / Unison
"Three Limericks"	p. 12	Triple / Mixolydian / Partner
"Turkey Struttin' 'Round"	p. 4	Duple / Mixolydian / Unison
"What Would the World Be Like Without Music?"	p. 14	Duple / Major / Combinable
"The Whistle"	p. 19	Duple / Major / Unison
"You Make Me Glad That I Know You"	p. 36	Duple / Major / Unison

A Nichol's Worth, Volume III .... pp. 1-31

"Be Thankful For Love"	p. 28	Duple / Major / Unison
"Cold Wind of Winter"	p. 8	Duple / Major / Unison
"Dancing Bear"	p. 13	Duple / Major / Unison
"Don't Be A Slob"	p. 9	Combined (Duple & Triple) / Lydian / Unison
"Do You Ever?"	p. 14	Triple / Major / Unison
"Elephants, Monkeys, and Leopards"	p. 5	Triple / Major / Combinable
"Farm, Farm, Farm, Farm"	p. 2	Duple / Major / Combinable
"The Grasswalker"	p. 22	Unusual (5/8) / Major / Combinable
"Gus"	p. 3	Triple / Dorian / Unison
"Had A Little Thought"	p. 20	Duple / Major / Partner
"I Love A Melody"	p. 21	Duple / Major / Partner
"It's All Pretend"	p. 10	Triple / Minor / Unison
"I Want To Be A Circus Clown"	p. 15	Triple / Mixolydian / Unison
"March"	p. 1	Duple / Major / Combinable
"The Middle of the Night"	p. 6	Duple / Phrygian / Unison
"Misery To A Kid"	p. 30	Duple / Major / Unison
"My Aminal"	p. 29	Duple / Minor / Unison
"My Secret Tree"	p. 24	Duple / Major / Unison
"Oh, I'll Build A Snowman"	p. 18	Triple / Minor / Partner
"Oh, Moe Is We"	p. 26	Duple / Major / Unison
"Old Folks"	p. 12	Duple / Major / Combinable
"Pancakes"	p. 25	Duple / Major / Unison
"Shiver"	p. 7	Duple / Major / Unison
"Song For Any Season"	p. 16	Duple / Mixolydian & Dorian / Countermelody
"Take A Look at Your Life"	p. 11	Unusual (7/8) / Major / Round
"We Share the World Together"	p. 4	Duple / Major / Combinable
"Why Don't They Feel Like Me"	p. 19	Triple / Minor / Partner

A Nichol's Worth, Volume IV .... pp. 1-39

"A Favorite Thing to Me"	p. 24	Duple / Major / Unison
"April Rain"	p. 16	Triple / Phrygian / Round
"Children Are Laughing"	p. 32	Duple / Major / Unison
"Come On and Laugh With Me"	p. 19	Duple / Major / Partner
"The Eefin' Song"	p. 28	Duple / Minor / Combinable
"February"	p. 1	Duple / Major / Unison
"I Can Feel the Beauty"	p. 17	Duple / Major / Unison
"I'd Like to Roller Skate on the Moon"	p. 38	Duple / Major / Unison
"I'm So Unhappy"	p. 18	Duple / Major / Partner
"It's Snowing"	p. 4	Triple / Major / Partner
"January"	p. 6	Duple / Major / Combinable
"Johnson Boys"	p. 30	Duple / Major / Countermelody
"Just Give Me a Cloudy Day"	p. 2	Duple / Major / Unison
"Let Me Be"	p. 27	Triple / Lydian / Countermelody
"Let's Play in the Snow"	p. 4	Triple / Major / Partner
"Magic Land"	p. 20	Duple / Major / Combinable
"Monkey Business"	p. 13	Duple / Mixolydian / Round
"My Little Friend"	p. 34	Duple / Major / Unison
"Oh, Yeah?"	p. 5	Triple / Dorian / Unison
"Rain"	p. 26	Triple / Major / Combinable
"Smile and Be Yourself"	p. 14	Duple / Major / Countermelody
"There Were Some Times"	p. 36	Duple / Major / Unison
"Things Are For Things"	p. 25	Unusual (Multi-Metric) / Major / Unison
"We Are Together"	p. 8	Duple / Major / Unison
"You'll Sound As Weird As Me"	p. 25	Triple / Multi-Tonal / Unison
"You Ought To"	p. 12	Triple / Minor / Unison
"You're As Good As All of the Rest"	p. 10	Triple / Dorian / Unison

Preschooler Movement with Instrumental Music

The Book of Movement Exploration: Can You Move Like This?

Feierabend, J., & Kahan, J. (2003). *The book of movement exploration: Can you move like this?* Chicago, IL: GIA Publications, Inc. ISBN 1-57999-264-1.

Feierabend, J. (2110). *First steps in classical music: Keeping the beat! (Compiled by John Feierabend)*. Chicago, IL: GIA Publications, Inc. CD#: CD-493

Book Contents

Theme 1: Awareness of Body Parts & Whole ....pp. 11-16

    1.1 Whole Body Movement .... p. 12
    1.2 Isolated Body Parts .... p. 13
    1.3 Leading with a Part .... p. 16
    1.4 Initiating with a Part .... p. 16

Theme 2: Awareness of Time ....pp. 17-18

    2.1 Quick and Slow Movement .... p. 18
    2.2 Clock Time .... p. 18

Theme 3: Awareness of Space ....pp. 21-28

    3.1 Personal Space and General Space .... p. 22
    3.2 Direct / Indirect Pathway (Straight / Twisted) .... p. 22
    3.3 Inward Movement (Narrow) .... p. 24
    3.4 Outward Movement (Wide) .... p. 25
    3.5 Direction of Movement .... p. 27
    3.6 Distance of Movement .... p. 28

Theme 4: Awareness of Levels ....pp. 21-32

    4.1 High / Middle / Low .... p. 32

Theme 5: Awareness of Weight .... pp. 35-37

    5.1 Heavy / Light .... p. 36
    5.2 Strong / Gentle .... p. 37
    5.3 Tense / Relaxed .... p. 37

Theme 6: Awareness of Locomotion .... p. 49

Theme 7: Awareness of Flow .... pp. 43-46

    7.1 Sudden / Sustained .... p. 44
    7.2 Sequential / Simultaneous .... p. 45
    7.3 Bound / Free .... p. 46

Theme 8: Awareness of Shape .... pp. 49-50

    8.1 Becoming Shapes .... p. 50

Theme 9: Awareness of Others .... pp. 53-57

    9.1 Partners .... p. 54
    9.2 Groups .... p. 57

Theme 10: Student Created Movement .... pp. 59-63

    10.1 Representative Movement .... p. 60
    10.2 Non-Representative Movement .... p. 63

CD Contents and Music Concepts

Excerpt time lengths range from 1:09 to 2:55:

1. Concerto No. 10 in C Major (Arcangelo Corelli).........Major / Duple / Tempo = MM132

2. Concerto No. 11 in Bb Flat Major: *Allemanda, Allegro* (Arcangelo Corelli)
....Major / Duple / Tempo = MM130

3. Concerto No. 12 in F Major (Arcangelo Corelli)
.... Major / Duple Compound / Tempo = MM132

4. Concert in F Major: *Giga, Allegro* (Arcangelo Corelli)
....Major / Triple / Tempo = MM126

5. Gloria in D, RV 589: *Domini Fili* (Antonio Vivaldi)
....Major / Triple / Tempo = MM126

6. Suite and Dances: *Premier et deuxiéme contredanse* (Jean-Philip Rameau)
....Major / Duple / Tempo = MM130

7. Suite No. 3 in D, BWV 1068: *Gigue* (J .S. Bach)
.... Major / Duple Compound / Tempo = MM120

8. Suite No. 4 in D, BWV 1069: *Gavotte* (J. S. Bach)
....Major / Duple / Tempo = MM136

9. Suite No. 4 in D, BWV 1069: *Rejouissance* (J. S. Bach)
....Major / Duple / Tempo = MM126

10. Suite No. 2 in b minor, BWV 1067: *Bourée I and II* (J. S. Bach)
.... Minor / Duple / Tempo = MM120

11. Suite No. 2 in b minor, BWV 1067: *Minuet* (J. S. Bach)
.... Minor / Triple / Tempo = MM132

12. Suite No. 2 in b minor, BWV 1067: Badinerie (J. S. Bach)
.... Minor / Duple / Tempo = MM126

13. Magnificat: Et exsultavit (J. S. Bach) .... Major / Triple / Tempo = MM122

14. Water Music: Allegro: (Gigue) (George Frideric Handel)
.... Major / Duple Compound / Tempo = MM136

15. Fireworks Music: Minuet II (George Frideric Handel)
.... Major / Triple / Tempo = MM132

16. Water Music: Minuet (George Frideric Handel) ...... Major / Triple / Tempo = MM124

17. Concerto grosso in D Major, Op. 1, No. 5: *Allegro* (Pietro Locatelli)
.... Major / Duple / Tempo = MM136

18. Concerto grosso in D Major, Op. 1, No. 9: *Allegro* (Pietro Locatelli)
.... Major / Triple / Tempo = MM136

19. Eine kliene Nachtmusik, K. 525: *Allegro* (Wolfgang Amadeus Mozart)
.... Major / Duple / Tempo = MM132

20. Eine kliene Nachtmusik, K. 525: *Rondo, Allegro* (Wolfgang Amadeus Mozart)
.... Major / Duple / Tempo = MM120

21. Symphony No. 40 in g minor, K. 550: *Allegro assai* (Wolfgang Amadeus Mozart)
.... Major / Duple / Tempo = MM126

22. Ballet Music from Faust: *Allegretto* (Charles Gounod)
.... Minor / Duple / Tempo = MM120

23. Gaîté Parisienne: Overture (Jacques Offenbach) ..... Major / Duple / Tempo = MM126

24. Gaîté Parisienne: *Guadrille* and *Allegro* (Jacques Offenbach)
.... Major / Duple / Tempo = MM120

25. Gaîté Parisienne: *Allegro* and *Allegro* (Jacques Offenbach)
.... Major / Duple / Tempo = MM136

26. Hungarian Dances: No. 18 (Johannes Brahms) .... Minor / Duple / Tempo = MM136

27. Swan Lake: Spanish Dance (Peter Ilyich Tchaikovsky)
.... Major / Triple / Tempo = MM124

28. The Nutcracker: Overture (Peter Ilyich Tchaikovsky)
....Major / Duple / Tempo = MM128

29. Ancient Airs and Dances: Suite No. 1: Baletto detto "Il Conte Orlando" (Ottorino Respighi) ....Major / Duple / Tempo = MM126

30. Ancient Airs and Dances: Suite No. 2: Laura Soave (Ottorino Respighi)
....Major / Duple / Tempo = MM126

31. Háry János Suite: Viennese Musical Clock (Zoltan Kodaly)
....Major / Duple / Tempo = MM128

32. Pulcinella Suite: *Allegro* (Igor Stravinsky) ....Major / Duple / Tempo = MM126

33. Symphony No. 1 in D Major: Gavotte: *Non troppo allegro* (Sergei Prokofiev)
....Major / Duple / Tempo = MM120

34. Rodeo: Hoe-Down (Aaron Copeland) ....Major / Duple / Tempo = MM128

35. Romeo and Juliet: Preparation for the Ball (Dmitry Kabalevsky)
....Major / Duple / Tempo = MM126

36. The Comedians: Epilogue (Dmitry Kabalevsky) ....Major / Duple / Tempo = MM126

Notes for
BOOK 2: TODDLERS

BITTY BOPS

BOOK 3: PRESCHOOLERS
PreK Music Curriculum for Ages 4 thru 5

How To Use *Bitty Bops—Preschoolers* Music Curriculum

There are four main sections to *Bitty Bops—Preschoolers* Music Curriculum.

PRESCHOOLERS LESSON STRUCTURE & ACTIVITIES EXPLAINED
(1) *Bitty Bops—Preschoolers* music teachers must first learn the Preschoolers Lesson Structure and explanation of Preschoolers Activities. **(See Document 21 and paragraphs in Document 24.)**

HOW PRESCHOOLERS LEARN MUSIC
(2) Dr. Edwin Gordon's research and publication explain how pre-K12 children learn, their responses, and how a teacher should interact with the student for each of the stages of:

    ACCULTURATION (Infants: Birth to Age 2-4)
    IMITATION (Toddlers: Ages 2-4 to 3-5)
    ASSIMILATION (Preschoolers: Ages 3-5 to 4-6)

All levels of *Bitty Bops* music teachers need to know what comprises these stages, how to recognize children's responses for each level, and how the *Bitty Bops* music teacher should interact rhythmically and tonally with the children on each level. For this level, *Bitty Bops—Preschoolers*, music teachers especially need to know the stages of ASSIMILATION (Preschoolers: Ages 3-5 to 4-6). **(See Document 22.)**

COMPILATION OF CURRICULAR MATERIALS
(3) *Bitty Bops—Preschoolers* music teachers should be thoroughly familiar with all the songs and activities so that Preschoolers may be taught according to their developmental and response stages.

    PRESCHOOLERS SONGS COLLECTION: These songs and activities, indexed by music activity categories, are compiled and field-tested by an experienced pre-K12 music teacher from more than a decade of teaching at this age level. **(See Document 24.)**

    MUSIC TOGETHER SONG COLLECTIONS: From Ken Guilmartin and Dr. Lillian Levinowitz, pre-K12 music experts at Rowan University. **(See Document 25.)**

Tambourine Song Collection	Sticks Song Collection
Fiddle Song Collection	Flute Song Collection
Triangle Song Collection	Summer Songs 1
Drum Song Collection	Summer Songs 2
Bongos Song Collection	Summer Songs 3
Maracas Song Collection	Babies
Bells Song Collection	Family Favorites Songbook for Teachers

    MUSIC PLAY: BOOK 1: From Dr. Gordon and his associates at Temple University and surrounding areas, this music book is created based on the music learning sequence Gordon research for pre-K12ers. **(See Document 26.)**

NICHOL'S WORTH: VOLUMES 1-2-3-4: A great collection of fun and humorous songs. These are witty, folk-like songs in four volumes, featuring all combinations of Meters (duple, triple, and multi-metric combined); Modes (Major, Minor, Dorian, Mixolydian, Phrygian, Lydian, and multi-tonal); in vocal textures (unison, combinable songs, partner songs, ostinatos, countermelodies, and rounds) that many other song collections neglect to include. **(See Document 27.)** (For the much-neglected Locrian mode, see the Knauss Music Curriculum, Book 1, pp. 50, 82-84. All modes may be sung in canon, see Knauss Music Curriculum, Book 3, pp. 18-20. For the Locrian mode, transpose the canon to the scale notes B to B: Ti-Do-Re-Mi-Fa-So-La-Ti.)

THE BOOK OF MOVEMENT EXPLORATION: CAN YOU MOVE LIKE THIS? Dr. John Feierabend has many years of research and experience with pre-K12 music teaching as well as expertly certified in the Kódaly music education approach. **(See Document 28.)**

FIRST STEPS IN CLASSICAL MUSIC: KEEPING THE BEAT! Dr. John Feierabend compiled an accompanying CD to the above book featuring many great classical works for children's exposure to classical styles. **(See Document 28.)**

PRESCHOOLERS MUSIC LESSON PLANS

(4) *Bitty Bops—Preschoolers* music teachers need to be familiar with all of the above information, songs, and activities, to the point of having them memorized so that they naturally flow out of the music teacher in smooth, well-transitioned, dove-tailed music lessons. See the lesson plan instructions and example music lesson plans for dovetailing and planning a balanced presentation and exposure to all Active Participations, Rhythm and Tonal Patterns, Song Categories, Meters, and Modes. **(See Document 23.)**

Contents for *Bitty Bops—Preschoolers*
(Documents 20-28)

	Page
Document 20: How to Use *Bitty Bops—Preschooler* Music Curriculum	120
Document 21: Preschoolers Lesson Structure and Activities Explained	123
Document 22: How Preschoolers Learn Music	125
Document 23: Preschoolers Music Lesson Plans	128
Document 24: Preschoolers Songs Notebook Index	137
Document 25: Preschoolers Music Together Books Index	158
Document 26: Preschoolers Music Play Book Index	173
Document 27: Preschoolers Nichol's Worth Books Index	177
Document 28: Preschoolers Movement Exploration and Keeping the Beat Index	182

Preschoolers Classes & Activities Explained
Age 4 thru 5

"Cardinal" Rules that must never be broken or neglected when teaching pre-K12 music classes:
1. Every song must have movement on the steady beat (except for purposeful interpretive movements). Always plan your movements. Also, copy any students' spontaneous movements.
2. All movements must exhibit a steady beat.
3. Male and female teachers alike must use their head voices so that the students learn to match in their light head voices. When all students are securely in tune, then the male teacher may use his lower voice and be certain that the students are aware of the octave transfer.
4. The teacher should never play an instrument to have students match pitches, because the transfer gap in timbre from instrument to voice is too wide. The teacher must always use voice to voice.
5. At the end of every singing song, the teacher sings the "Sol-Do" of the song with hand motions—palms pointing down at chest level (Sol) and ending on the floor or waist level (Do). Pause for two seconds after the Sol, to allow for students to respond if they wish with the Do.

Each Preschoolers Lesson Plan should contain the following, depending on class length:
1. Hello / Goodbye songs
2. Stationary movement songs / body awareness songs and activities
3. Large gross motor activity / traveling movement—possibly using manipulatives, such as hoops and scarves
4. Steady beat activities to utilizing instruments—(sticks, drums, jingles, shakers, scarves)
5. Songs focused on vocal responses / call and response activities (Orff xylophones / resonator bars)
6. Stories / Story songs / Sound stories (Orff xylophones)
7. Focused listening sounds
8. Rhythmic and tonal patterns, both simple and complex
9. Group dance activity
10. From one music activity to the next, music concepts dovetailed (see Lesson Plan chart).
11. For the music learning stages of preschoolers, see ASSIMILATION stages in the chart of How Preschoolers Learn Music (see Document 22).
12. Each class should contain approximately 12-14 songs including hello/goodbye songs, dependent on time length of class. The use of the word parent in the follow paragraphs denotes caregiver, babysitter, family relative, or anyone who regularly brings the preschooler to each class.

Repetition. Repetition the most important aspect of learning in early childhood music. Songs are repeated from week to week, but varied with different instruments and movements. The majority of each class is repeated familiar songs and activities, with only a few being introduced as new. When new ones are consistently repeated, they too become familiar.

Actions Not Explanations. The teacher begins each class with singing, ends with singing, and even sings all 4-word-or-less instructions between activities (only if instructions are absolutely needed). In preschool ages, children do not learn with linguistic explanations—they learn experientially. Only parents need explanations, such as the preschool stages of learning (see ASSIMILATION stages in chart of How Preschoolers Learn Music (see Document 22), or reminders why their participation is the superior modeling for their preschooler. When parents need explanations or reminders that they are active participants all the time, provide these apart from the flow of the lesson. Parents should sing every song the same as the teacher, because preschoolers need the emotional connection of the parent voice that they have been listening to since before they were born. Music is learned in the same way as language (Suzuki's "mother tongue" concept). So it is because we speak to preschoolers, regardless of their ability to answer or understand, to immerse them in unlimited exposure. In this way, preschoolers will acquire the sounds and rhythms. Usually beginning in Kindergarten or after they begin to read and write in the language.

Smooth Transitions. When moving from song to song, either sing a transition melodic phrase, or a clean-up song. Do not speak instructions. Keep the music ongoing. Think about what is coming next and prepare preschoolers and parents for the activity with movement to do together. "March with me," or "caw like a crow," or just jump right into the next song or activity. Don't stop the music, but rather keep songs flowing from one to the next. If a child does not want to "clean up," they will eventually copy the others. When you, the teacher, give out the next object for the next activity, you can trade them objects without saying a word or bringing attention to their negative behavior. In this way, always promote a positive atmosphere.

Playing Not Performing. Real learning that will stick, will happen when preschoolers feel comfortable in their learning environment, when there is repetition, and when they are emotionally connected to the activity through laughter and enjoyment. Growing a relationship with that preschooler can happen through music class, which of course is inherently fun, but a child will also naturally gravitate to someone who will "play" with them. An effective early childhood teacher is one who has a playful spirit and is thoroughly animated. Children learn through play and are naturally playful beings. They will respond to adults who are authentically silly right along with them. Teachers need to find that playful spirit that feels natural to them.

Acceptance Without Expectations. Children are different learners. Some are active participants and some do not participate at all but they are absorbing the class and its activities like a sponge, regardless of what they are doing on the exterior. What they do in class, most likely they will imitate at home where they are most comfortable. We take the children, where they are, and whatever type of learner they are, and accept them as they are. Early childhood music education, informal music education, is not at all like formal music education in K-12, where responses are expected. The teacher must be aware that participation or responses may or may not happen depending on the learning stage of the preschooler (see ASSIMILATION stages in chart of How Preschoolers Learn Music (see Document 22).

Parent Education. Parents should be reminded that they are to be their preschooler's example. Parents must be involved, not sitting or standing as silent observers outside the activity circle. Preschoolers need to see that their parents value music and that they lead by modeling, showing the joy of music even when the preschooler is not participating. Parent socializing should not happen during class, and should be addressed either through an initial handout explaining class procedure and parental expectations, or verbal reminders. Remind the parents to turn their "talking" voices off as they enter the room. Parents may also need to be reminded that the music curriculum is developmentally geared to the preschool child so repetition is a key component. Preschoolers are emotionally connected to their parents and their voices, so when modeling, remind parents that it doesn't matter how well or perfectly they sound. It is primarily the fact that it is THEIR sound their preschooler will respond to and connect with. This ensures that the best learning will happen!

How Preschoolers Learn Music

Gordon, E.E. (2003). *A music learning theory for newborn and young children*. Chicago, IL: GIA Publications, Inc. ISBN: 1-57999-259-5.

"Audiation takes place when one hears and comprehends music silently, the sound of the music no longer being or never having been physically present. In contrast, aural perception takes place when one hears music when its sound is physically present." (p. 25).

"Audition is to music what thought is to language. Audiating while you are performing music is like thinking while you are speaking, and audiating while listening to music is like thinking about what persons have said and are saying as you are listening to them speak." (p.25).

"Audiation is the basis of music aptitude." (p. 25).

Music learning continues for Ages 3-5 to 4-6 with the ASSIMILATION stages, after sequentially developing through the ACCULTURATION and IMITATION stages. (See the following ASSIMILATION stages.)

TYPES	CHILD'S RESPONSES	TEACHER'S INTERACTION
3. ASSIMILATION: Ages 3-5 to 4-6: participates with conscious thought focused on self (p. 42) ASSIMILATION is the stage in which children progress from imitation what they hear in patterns or what they see in breathing and movement without meaning (much like imitation of individual words when they are first learning to speak without knowing syntactical organization of the words) to assimilating pitch, rhythm, breathing, and movement into a syntax to create musical understanding. Children learn to perform patterns with further precision as they coordinate and assimilate the imitation of those patterns with their breathing and movement. Children in Assimilation are able to perform more accurately, using their voice or a musical instrument, together in groups as well as solo, and they are able to adjust their pitch and rhythm to make accommodations in performing in groups with others for a unified musical whole.	3.A. INTROSPECTION: Child recognizes the lack of coordination between singing, chanting, breathing, and movement (p. 42) Children become aware of the way they are breathing and moving their bodies in coordination with their singing of tonal patterns and their chanting of rhythm patterns. (p. 46) CHILD'S RESPONSES OR REACTIONS TO MUSIC: Child engages in the process of imitation, but indicates that (s)he realizes his/her breathing and moving are not coordinated with his/her singing by looking at the adult who initiated patterns or at his/her own parent. After beginning to perform a tonal pattern without a breath, a child sill stop him/herself and begin again, trying to breathe before singing., but his/her movements may not be consistently coordinated with his/her breathing and singing.	TEACHER'S INTERACTION WITH CHILD'S RESPONSES: Continue structure informal guidance during arpeggioed, tonal and rhythm Assimilation pattern guidance and classroom activities. Continue to model a deep, full breath preceding each tonal pattern. Be certain to present to children all possible arpeggioed tonic and dominant tonal patterns in Major and Harmonic Minor tonalities to increase their tonal pattern vocabularies. Be sure to present to children all possible four macro beat rhythm patterns in Usual Duple and Usual Triple meters to increase their rhythm pattern vocabularies. Encourage children with suggestions such as "move like this" or "watch me." Stand and engage your whole body in continuous, flowing movements. Structure opportunities for repeating activities that emphasize moving, breathing, and performing tonal and rhythm patterns. At no time tell the child that his/her tonal or rhythm patterns are incorrect or that (s)he is not coordinating his/her breathing and moving with singing. Encourage spontaneous songs, chants, and movements created by child. Continue to perform music in a variety of tonalities and meters while moving with continuous flow.

TYPES	CHILD'S RESPONSES	TEACHER'S INTERACTION
	3.B. COORDINATION:

Child coordinates singing and chanting with breathing and movement (p. 42)

Children actually learn how, on a conscious level, to coordinate with some precision their singing and chanting of tonal patterns and rhythm patterns with their breathing and the weight and flow of their body movements. (p. 47)

CHILD'S RESPONSES OR REACTIONS TO MUSIC:

After child realizes (s)he has not taken a breath before his/her tonal pattern, (s)he becomes more consistent in his/her attempts to coordinate breathing and moving with singing.

Child continues to improve the accuracy with which (s)he performs tonal and rhythm patterns. | TEACHER'S INTERACTION WITH CHILD'S RESPONSES:

Continue structure informal guidance during arpeggioed, tonal and rhythm Assimilation pattern guidance and classroom activities.

Continue to model a deep, full breath preceding each tonal or rhythm pattern.

At this time, continue to introduce and repeat activities that encourage child to breathe consistently, such as hopping or jumping before singing or chanting and then immediately engage child in moving with continuous flow while (s)he performs tonal or rhythm patterns.

If children are still unable to perform complete tonal patterns while moving with continuous flow, invite them to sing only the resting tone as you present two, then three, then four note patterns to them.

Encourage spontaneous songs, chants, and movements created by child.

Continue to perform music in a variety of tonalities and meters while moving with continuous flow.

Perform tonal patterns in tonalities other than Major and Harmonic Minor.

Make recommendations about formal instruction in music when child has phased through this Stage 3.B. in both tonal and rhythm preparatory audiation. |

Gordon, E.E. (2003). *A music learning theory for newborn and young children.* Chicago, IL: GIA Publications, Inc. ISBN: 1-57999-259-5. (summarized from pp. 42, 46-47).

Preschoolers Music Lesson Plans
Guidelines for Planning

(1) Whatever you choose as the "Hello Song" and "Goodbye Song" for the first class of the semester, keep those songs consistent for the whole semester. Change the "Hello" and "Goodbye" songs to different ones for a following semester.

(2) Follow careful Dovetailing of music concepts from activity to activity so that something remains familiar from activity to activity in each lesson—thus controlling the number of music concepts that are new from activity to activity. Also note the changing of music concepts down the column. (See the Infant Lesson Plans, Document 03, for how they are repeated or "dovetailed" from activity to activity.)

(3) Carefully plan the number of familiar activities, as opposed to new activities, from lesson to lesson. Repeat a majority of familiar songs from the previous lesson(s) and use a small number of new songs. (See the arrows that point forward into the next lesson plan. These arrows indicate the songs that are carried as familiar over into the next lesson plan.)

(4) Be sure to include something of Listening, Singing, Chanting, Moving, Playing, Performing, Creating, and Improvising in some way throughout the progress of each lesson. (See the third column labeled Dovetailing of Mode / Meter / Specialty.)

(5) Choose 3-4 Duple and Triple Rhythms and insert into the Lesson Plan where appropriate. Choose 3-4 Major and Minor Tonal Patterns and insert into the Lesson Plan where appropriate. Chant on neutral syllable "ba" for rhythm and sing on neutral syllable "nu" or "loo" for tonal. Perform the rhythm and tonal patterns looking directly at Preschooler. Pause a second or two after each to give preschooler time to respond if (s)he desires. Whatever response is given, immediately copy it back to the preschooler. If most of the preschoolers echo respond with the rhythm or tonal pattern presented, this indicates to the teacher that the rhythm syllables or tonal syllables may be used instead of the neutral syllables. (These rhythms and tonal patterns are found in the Knauss Music Curriculum, Book 1A.)

(6) Plan for music activities that are at the Preschoolers' level as well as music that is beyond the Preschoolers' level, the same as parents use single words or short phrases to their preschoolers, as well as speak adult-level coherent paragraphs with complex words and sentence structures, even second languages.

(7) Include listening and moving to an instrumental selection in each lesson—whether popular, classical, cultural, or whatever.

(8) Because music potential is genius level at birth, and slowly declines from there, always provide the preschoolers with the greatest exposure to all kinds and levels and complexity of music—nothing is outside their exposure, absorption, imitation, and assimilation abilities at this age.

Tracking the Content of Preschoolers Lesson Plans

When planning the sequence of each next lesson from the one before, the goal is for an evenly varied musical exposure and experience across each class semester.

	Active Participations				Rhythm & Tonal Patterns			Songs															
								Song Categories							Meters			Modes					
	Singing / Chanting	Moving	Playing / Performing	Creating / Improvising	Duple Rhythm Patterns	Triple Rhythm Patterns	Tonal Patterns	Stationary Movement / Finger Play / Body Aware	Large Gross Motor Activity with Movement	Vocal Response / Call and Response Activity	Group Dance Activity	Travel Movement / Large Gross Motor	Steady Beat Activity / Instrument Song	Musical Story / Story Song / Sound Story	Duple Meter	Triple Meter	Unusual Meter	Major (Ionian)	Minor (Aeolian)	Mixolydian	Dorian	Lydian	Phrygian	Locrian
Lesson 1																								
Lesson 2																								
Lesson 3																								
Lesson 4																								
Lesson 5																								
Lesson 6																								
Lesson 7																								
Lesson 8																								
Lesson 9																								
Lesson 10																								
Lesson 11																								
Lesson 12																								
Lesson 13																								
Lesson 14																								
Lesson 15																								
TOTALS (Goal is for an evenly varied musical exposure and experience across each class semester)																								

Preschoolers Music Lesson Plan 1

Choose 3-4 Duple and Triple Rhythms and insert into the Lesson Plan where appropriate.
Choose 3-4 Major and Minor Tonal Patterns and insert into the Lesson Plan where appropriate.

CATEGORY	MATERIALS	DOVETAILING OF MODE / METER / SPECIALTY	ACTIVITY
Hello Song	"Hello Song" Music Together—Sticks Song Collection, p. 13	Major Duple Singing & Pat / Clap the Duple Meter	Sit in a circle and sway back and forth gently on the macrobeats—perform steady beats
Stationary Movement / Finger Play / Body Awareness			
Large Gross Motor Activity / Traveling Movement			
Vocal Response / Call and Respond			
Group Dance Activities			
Travel Movement / Large Gross Motor			
Steady Beat Activity / Instrument Song			
Musical Story / Story Song / Sound Story			
Goodbye Song	"Goodbye, So Long, Farewell" by Ken Guilmartin Music Together—Sticks, p. 45	Major Triple Swaying & Pat / Clap / Clap the Triple Meter	Back to sitting in a circle—use each of the preschooler's and parent's names to sing goodbye—sway a goodbye hand to the triple meter

(There are only 9 activities above; 12-14 are to be planned by repeating categories.)

Preschoolers Music Lesson Plan 2

Choose 3-4 Duple and Triple Rhythms and insert into the Lesson Plan where appropriate.
Choose 3-4 Major and Minor Tonal Patterns and insert into the Lesson Plan where appropriate.

CATEGORY	MATERIALS	DOVETAILING OF MODE / METER / SPECIALTY	ACTIVITY
Hello Song	"Hello Song" Music Together—Sticks Song Collection, p. 13	Major Duple Singing & Pat / Clap the Duple Meter	Sit in a circle and sway back and forth gently on the macrobeats—perform steady beats
Stationary Movement / Finger Play / Body Awareness			
Large Gross Motor Activity / Traveling Movement			
Vocal Response / Call and Respond			
Group Dance Activities			
Travel Movement / Large Gross Motor			
Steady Beat Activity / Instrument Song			
Musical Story / Story Song / Sound Story			
Goodbye Song	"Goodbye, So Long, Farewell" by Ken Guilmartin Music Together—Sticks, p. 45	Major Triple Swaying & Pat / Clap / Clap the Triple Meter	Back to sitting in a circle—use each of the preschooler's and parent's names to sing goodbye—sway a goodbye hand to the triple meter

(There are only 9 activities above; 12-14 are to be planned by repeating categories.)

Preschoolers Music Lesson Plan 3

Choose 3-4 Duple and Triple Rhythms and insert into the Lesson Plan where appropriate.
Choose 3-4 Major and Minor Tonal Patterns and insert into the Lesson Plan where appropriate.

CATEGORY	MATERIALS	DOVETAILING OF MODE / METER / SPECIALTY	ACTIVITY
Hello Song	"Hello Song" Music Together—Sticks Song Collection, p. 13	Major Duple Singing & Pat / Clap the Duple Meter	Sit in a circle and sway back and forth gently on the macrobeats—perform steady beats
Stationary Movement / Finger Play / Body Awareness			
Large Gross Motor Activity / Traveling Movement			
Vocal Response / Call and Respond			
Group Dance Activities			
Travel Movement / Large Gross Motor			
Steady Beat Activity / Instrument Song			
Musical Story / Story Song / Sound Story			
Goodbye Song	"Goodbye, So Long, Farewell" by Ken Guilmartin Music Together—Sticks, p. 45	Major Triple Swaying & Pat / Clap / Clap the Triple Meter	Back to sitting in a circle—use each of the preschooler's and parent's names to sing goodbye—sway a goodbye hand to the triple meter

(There are only 9 activities above; 12-14 are to be planned by repeating categories.)

Preschoolers Music Lesson Plan 4

Choose 3-4 Duple and Triple Rhythms and insert into the Lesson Plan where appropriate.
Choose 3-4 Major and Minor Tonal Patterns and insert into the Lesson Plan where appropriate.

CATEGORY	MATERIALS	DOVETAILING OF MODE / METER / SPECIALTY	ACTIVITY
Hello Song	"Hello Song" Music Together—Sticks Song Collection, p. 13	Major Duple Singing & Pat / Clap the Duple Meter	Sit in a circle and sway back and forth gently on the macrobeats—perform steady beats
Stationary Movement / Finger Play / Body Awareness			
Large Gross Motor Activity / Traveling Movement			
Vocal Response / Call and Respond			
Group Dance Activities			
Travel Movement / Large Gross Motor			
Steady Beat Activity / Instrument Song			
Musical Story / Story Song / Sound Story			
Goodbye Song	"Goodbye, So Long, Farewell" by Ken Guilmartin Music Together—Sticks, p. 45	Major Triple Swaying & Pat / Clap / Clap the Triple Meter	Back to sitting in a circle—use each of the preschooler's and parent's names to sing goodbye—sway a goodbye hand to the triple meter

(There are only 9 activities above; 12-14 are to be planned by repeating categories.)

Preschoolers Music Lesson Plan 5

Choose 3-4 Duple and Triple Rhythms and insert into the Lesson Plan where appropriate.
Choose 3-4 Major and Minor Tonal Patterns and insert into the Lesson Plan where appropriate.

CATEGORY	MATERIALS	DOVETAILING OF MODE / METER / SPECIALTY	ACTIVITY
Hello Song	"Hello Song" Music Together—Sticks Song Collection, p. 13	Major Duple Singing & Pat / Clap the Duple Meter	Sit in a circle and sway back and forth gently on the macrobeats—perform steady beats
Stationary Movement / Finger Play / Body Awareness			
Large Gross Motor Activity / Traveling Movement			
Vocal Response / Call and Respond			
Group Dance Activities			
Travel Movement / Large Gross Motor			
Steady Beat Activity / Instrument Song			
Musical Story / Story Song / Sound Story			
Goodbye Song	"Goodbye, So Long, Farewell" by Ken Guilmartin Music Together—Sticks, p. 45	Major Triple Swaying & Pat / Clap / Clap the Triple Meter	Back to sitting in a circle—use each of the preschooler's and parent's names to sing goodbye—sway a goodbye hand to the triple meter

(There are only 9 activities above; 12-14 are to be planned by repeating categories.)

Preschoolers Music Lesson Plan 6

Choose 3-4 Duple and Triple Rhythms and insert into the Lesson Plan where appropriate.
Choose 3-4 Major and Minor Tonal Patterns and insert into the Lesson Plan where appropriate.

CATEGORY	MATERIALS	DOVETAILING OF MODE / METER / SPECIALTY	ACTIVITY
Hello Song	"Hello Song" Music Together—Sticks Song Collection, p. 13	Major Duple Singing & Pat / Clap the Duple Meter	Sit in a circle and sway back and forth gently on the macrobeats—perform steady beats
Stationary Movement / Finger Play / Body Awareness			
Large Gross Motor Activity / Traveling Movement			
Vocal Response / Call and Respond			
Group Dance Activities			
Travel Movement / Large Gross Motor			
Steady Beat Activity / Instrument Song			
Musical Story / Story Song / Sound Story			
Goodbye Song	"Goodbye, So Long, Farewell" by Ken Guilmartin Music Together—Sticks, p. 45	Major Triple Swaying & Pat / Clap / Clap the Triple Meter	Back to sitting in a circle—use each of the preschooler's and parent's names to sing goodbye—sway a goodbye hand to the triple meter

(There are only 9 activities above; 12-14 are to be planned by repeating categories.)

Preschoolers Music Lesson Plan 7

Choose 3-4 Duple and Triple Rhythms and insert into the Lesson Plan where appropriate.
Choose 3-4 Major and Minor Tonal Patterns and insert into the Lesson Plan where appropriate.

CATEGORY	MATERIALS	DOVETAILING OF MODE / METER / SPECIALTY	ACTIVITY
Hello Song	"Hello Song" Music Together—Sticks Song Collection, p. 13	Major Duple Singing & Pat / Clap the Duple Meter	Sit in a circle and sway back and forth gently on the macrobeats—perform steady beats
Stationary Movement / Finger Play / Body Awareness			
Large Gross Motor Activity / Traveling Movement			
Vocal Response / Call and Respond			
Group Dance Activities			
Travel Movement / Large Gross Motor			
Steady Beat Activity / Instrument Song			
Musical Story / Story Song / Sound Story			
Goodbye Song	"Goodbye, So Long, Farewell" by Ken Guilmartin Music Together—Sticks, p. 45	Major Triple Swaying & Pat / Clap / Clap the Triple Meter	Back to sitting in a circle—use each of the preschooler's and parent's names to sing goodbye—sway a goodbye hand to the triple meter

(There are only 9 activities above; 12-14 are to be planned by repeating categories.)

Preschoolers Songs Collection
Indexed by Music Activity
Ages 4 thru 5

NOTE: The follow songs are organized by suggested activity categories. The music for them may be found in well-known publications or on the Internet.

Hello / Goodbye Songs. Each lesson should contain a "Hello Song" and a "Good-bye Song." These songs may be two different ones, one for Hello and one for Goodbye, or they may be the Hello song with the lyrics changed for Goodbye. These remain the same for the entire class semester. During the Hello and Goodbye songs, each child's name is sung with an activity to keep the steady beat. Singing hello to every child is a wonderful way to affirm his/her presence as an individual and as a member of the group. After a few weeks, when the children have warmed up to the activities and to the environment, ask them for their ideas on how they would like to be greeted. This allows for the "emerging independent 3-4 year-old" to appear. Many children will respond with a motion of clapping, tapping, pointing, etc., instead of responding verbally. To encourage the verbal aspect and language development, ask them what they usually call that motion. Upon hearing the answer, it is repeated to the class and then sung in the song. This simple activity signals the start of the class, recognizes the specialness of each child, and gives each child the opportunity to direct the actions of the entire class through the use of language.

    Hello Song (Music Together-Bongos) CD #1 .... Duple / Major

    Goodbye, So Long, Farewell (Music Together-Bongos) .... Triple / Major

Familiar songs and change words such as:
Dem Bones
Are You Sleeping?
Alphabet Song
Farmer in the Dell
Skip To My Lou
Old McDonald Had a Farm
Row Row Row Your Boat
Yankee Doodle
Go Tell Aunt Rhodie
The More We Get Together
Clap, Clap, Clap Your Hands
This is The Way We Wash Our Clothes
Mary Had A Little Lamb
Good Night Ladies

Stationary Movement Songs / Body Awareness Songs and Activities. These songs and activities allow for fine motor and language development growth opportunities. Movement and learning are linked in younger children. Stationary movement activities, such as clapping, pounding, stamping, jumping, hopping, and balancing movements, allow each child to explore what they can do with their body while remaining is a stable position. Additionally, stationary movement activities allow children to explore spatial concepts, such as high, low, in, out, and through, as well as "my space" and "your space." One goal of these movement activities is to allow each child the opportunity to gain control of his/her body and to have movement be the result of "thought" as opposed to being simply a reflex.

All The Little Ducklings (Music Copy).. Duple / Major

By 'n' By (Music Together-Bells) jingles to count fingers/xylophones
.... Duple / Major

Clap Your Hands (Music Together-Drums) tap body parts then add instruments
.... Duple / Mixolydian on D

(or use the Music Copy in the Notebook).. Duple / Major

Down In The Meadow (Music Copy) pat steady beats and have children create new animal verses... Duple / Dorian on F

Eensy, Weensey Spider (Music Together-Bongo) CD#15 .... Triple / Major

Five Little Mice (Music Together-Maracas) then use instruments to be mice scampering away .... Duple Rhythmic Chant

Go Round The Mountain (can also use by tapping on different body parts) – see link below
http://www.abcteacherguides.com/Media/TakeHomePages/ABC_LL/OandA/OandA_THP_1_2.pdf ....

Hands On Shoulders poem (Music Copy from Poems and Fingerplays)
.... Duple or Triple Rhythmic Chant

Head, Shoulders, Knees, Toes song (Music Copy from Poems and Fingerplays)
.... Duple / Major

Hop Ol' Squirrel (Music Together-Maracas) do the motions of squirrel before adding instruments .... Duple / Major

I've Got The Rhythm In My Head (Music Together-Fiddle) .... Duple / Major

Jack Be Nimble (Music Copy)... Duple / Major

Jack Be Nimble (Music Together-Maracas) .... Triple Rhythmic Chant

Jim Along Josie (Music Together-Flutes) .... Duple / Major

Let us Chase The Squirrel (Music Copy).. Duple / Major

Open and Shut Them (Music Together-Bongos) CD#4 .... Duple / Major

Russian Folk Song (Music Together-Maracas) also known as May There Always Be Sunshine (rocking song) .... Duple / Major

See How I'm Jumping (Music Together-Bongos) .... Duple / Minor

She'll Be Comin' Round The Mountain (Music Together-Bongos) .... Duple / Major

Six Little Ducks (Music Copy) use with motions then ask for vocal response on the quacks .... Duple / Major

Ten Fingers (Music Together-Triangle) .... Duple Rhythmic Chant

That's A Mighty Pretty Motion (Music Copy) have children create their own motion as well .... Duple / Major

The Snail and The Mouse (Music Together-Drums) .... Duple Rhythmic Chant

There's A Little Wheel a-Turnin' (Music Together-Flutes) .... Duple / Major

This Little Light of Mine (Music Together-Fiddle) .... Duple / Major

This Old Man (Music Together-Bongos) CD#8 .... Duple / Major

Two Little Blackbirds (Music Together-Triangle) CD#26 .... Duple / Major

Two Red Apples poem (Music Copy from Poems and Fingerplays)
 .... Duple or Triple Rhythmic Chant

William, He Had Seven Sons (Music copy) .... Duple / Minor

Vocal Response / Call and Respond Activities. (Orff xylophones, resonator bars). These songs and activities encourage a response from the child, but responses may or may not be given, depending on the learning stage of the child (see ASSIMILATION stages in the Chart of How Preschoolers (Pre-K12ers) Learn Music). These activities create opportunities for the non-verbal or shy child to use his/her voice as well as develop the child's singing voice. The songs are first sung as an example and the response is taught by rote. Responses may or may not be given by the student. Parents can easily be the echo example for any non-responding child. Praise any response from the child. Once songs are learned, resonator bars or glockenspiels can be added to keep the steady beat using tones from the song's chords or melody. These songs and activities can include not only sung responses, but responding with farm and animal sounds, or tonal patterns that are echoed. In order to develop independent musicianship, the goal is to have the child always singing with the light quality and in the higher register that is referred to the singing voice, not the lower speaking voice. A child's singing can be assessed with solo opportunity songs. Always use the higher light register voice when singing as an example and use much inflection in the voice. Glockenspiels, resonator bars, and xylophones are wonderful pitch models, and are easy for children to play for providing a beautiful, simple accompaniment to many songs and stories. They can help establish the "home tone"—Do—as well as the teacher singing Sol-Do after each song or activity. These instruments can also help in teaching easy solfége patterns. Glockenspiels, resonator bars, and xylophones are used to teach simple music concepts, such as high and low, up and down, and steady beat, as well as developing fine motor skills. These instruments also help the children, with their imaginations, to bring story songs to life.

Aiken Drum (Music Copy) Use drums in creative ways to help keep the beat .... Duple / Major

Bird Song (Music Together-Triangles) CD#6-– resonator bars .... Triple / Phrygian on C

Bow Wow Wow (Music copy) resonator bars .... Duple / Major

By 'n' By (Music Together-Bells) jingles to count fingers/xylophones/children sing their number as solo.. Duple / Major

Ding Dong, Ding Dong (Music Together-Tambourine) echo with children—use with resonator bars/glocks.. Duple / Major / Tonal Round

Doggie, Doggie (music copy) Resonator bars/echo response/game ...... Duple / Major

Doodle (Music Together-Maracas) add resonator bars .... Duple / Minor

Down Comes Johnny (Music Copy) Use as game: http://www.stringskeysandmelodies.com/2012/08/more-fun-with-boomwhackers-down-comes.html.. Duple / Major

Dum Ditty Dum (Music Together-Flutes) resonator bars & echo each line with verses given .... Duple / Major

Fireworks (Music Together-Bongos) CD#9 –vocal exploration and scarves .... Triple Rhythmic Chant

Five Green and Speckled Frogs (Music Copy)-vocal response on sounds and drums .... Duple / Major

Good Day or When Ducks Get Up In The Morning (Music Copy) use with resonators or xylophones: http://www.nancymusic.com/Ducksplay.htm............... Triple / Major

Hill and Gully Rider(Music Copy) drums/sticks or resonator bars .... Duple / Major

If Your Happy and You Know It (Music Copy) .... Duple / Major

John The Rabbit (Music Together-Drum) .... Duple / Major

Li'L 'Liza Jane / Funga Alafia (Music Together-Bongs) CD#21 –vocal with resonator bars.. Duple / Major / Partner Songs

Lucy Locket (Music copy) Solo response/game .... Duple / Major

My Little Rooster (Music Copy) http://web.lyon.edu/wolfcollection/songs/riddleilove1260.html (listen to the recording from this site) Use different percussion instruments for each animal .... Triple / Major

No More Pie (Music Together-Fiddle) vocal with resonator bars .... Duple / Minor Blues

Old Blue (Music Together-Triangles) CD#27.......................... Duple / Mixolydian on D

Old Jeremiah or Jumpin' Jeremiah (Music Copy) use with resonator bars .... Triple / Minor

One Little Owl (Music Together-Tambourine) use with resonator bars

....Duple / Minor

....Duple / Major

Pease Porridge Hot (Music Together-Maracas)..........................Duple Rhythmic Chant

Round Robin (Music Together-Tambourine) use with resonators or even sticks, echo sing.. Duple / Major / Tonal Round

Sandpiper (Music Together-Flutes) rewritten as The Echo resonator bars or glocks
....Duple / Major

She'll Be Comin' Round The Mountain (Music Together-Bongos) vocal special effects
....Duple / Major

Six Little Ducks (Music Copy) Use for vocal response on the quacks and use resonator bars or Glockenspiels... Duple / Major

The Cuckoo (Music Copy) resonator bars/echo response .... Duple / Major

Twinkle, Twinkle (resonator bars or little choir bells) sing and play their bell note
....Duple / Major

Who Are You? (Music Copy) solo singing opportunity .... Duple / Major

Who's Got A Fishpole? (Music Copy) Add percussion sound (sticks) on the echo and act it out as you sing .... Duple / Major

Yoo Hoo (Music Copy) Resonator bars/echo response .... Duple / Major

Group Dance Activities. Dance activity songs can help develop large gross motor skills, as well as coordination and spatial awareness. Circle dance activities encourage a sense of community and cooperation where everyone moves together. They are joyous ways to experience melody, rhythm, and form (the organization of the music). Many singing games take on the shape of a circle, providing both parent and child the sense of community and energy that comes from being part of a group. Circle dance activities encourage a sense of community and cooperation where everyone plays together. The songs are sung and danced illustrating while singing or giving a quick heads up to the movement to come. Two well-known songs for dancing are London Bridge and Ring Around the Rosie.

Billy, Billy (Music Copy)... Duple / Major

Blue Bird (Music Copy) .... Duple / Major

Bow Belinda (Music Copy) .... Duple / Major

Dancing With Teddy (Music Together-Maracas) .... Triple / Major

Down The River (Music Copy) partner dance; movement from one side of room to the opposite.. Triple / Major

Everybody Loves Saturday Night (Music Together-Drums)
....Duple / Major

Goin' To Boston (Music Together-Fiddle).............................Duple / Mixolydian on C

Halloween Hokey Pokey: http://www.preschooleducation.com/shalloween.shtml
.... Duple / Major

Here We Go Looby Loo (Music Copy) .... Triple / Major

Here We Go Round the Mulberry Bush (Music Copy): http://www.youtube.com/watch?v=lr2PUHiw8Ek circle dance or move around hoops
.... Duple / Major

In And Out the Dusky Bluebells (Music Copy) words only-to learn it see website below: http://dailyrhymetime.wordpress.com/2012/05/07/in-and-out-the-dusky-bluebells/.. Duple / Major

Li'L 'Liza Jane (Music Together-Bongs) CD#21........................ Duple / Major

Little Bird, Go Through My Window (Music Copy): http: www.youtube.com/watch?v=GVQdC8YrrZI............................ Duple & Triple / Major

London Bridge (Mother Goose Club)....................................... Duple / Major

Mariá Isabel (Music Together-Triangles) CD#18 .... Duple / Major

Mountain Dew (Music Together-Bongo) CD#16 .... Triple / Major

Old Brass Wagon (Music Together-Tambourine) .... Duple / Major

Palo, Palo (Music Together-Bongo) CD#10 –treat like conga line .... Duple / Major

Rig-a-Jig-Jig (Mother Goose Club)... Triple / Major

Rig-a-Jig-Jig (Music Copy) .... Duple / Major

Ring Around The Rosie (Music Copy)...................................... Duple / Major

Shake Those Simmons Down (Music Copy) can also use scarves or shakers
.... Duple / Major

Shoo Fly (Music Copy) .... Duple / Major

Shoo Fly, Don't Bother Me (Music Together-Bongos)............. Duple / Major

Skip To My Lou (Music Together-Triangles) CD#7................... Duple / Major

The Noble Duke of York (Music Copy)..................................... Triple / Major

Large Gross Motor Activity / Traveling Movement. These are songs that are active and have the children up and moving through space. These songs will improve a child's coordination, balance, and spatial awareness. These songs can be songs about different types of movement, such as jumping, marching, twirling, crawling, skipping, etc., or could be songs that can use hoops to jump into or crawl through. These songs can be first sung stationary or using body percussion. Then they can be sung with traveling movements or manipulatives, such as hoops and scarves. Scarves are most often used to promote vocal inflection; to exercise the vocal muscle to stretch way up high and then down low. Scarves help to demonstrate fluid and sustained movements, and teach directionality. Hoops are used to teach spatial concepts, such as around, in, out, and through. Movement songs are exciting and energizing experiences for children that combine moving their various body parts in specific ways with the added challenge of moving through space. These traveling movement activities not only challenge children to control their bodies, but also to understand "their space" in relation to other class members. These large motor movement songs also help children to be able to stop and start movements with ease, and understand spatial concepts, such as in and out, directionality opposites, and high and low. These songs and activities are a great in the beginning of the class after the Hello Song because they are fun and energizing, and since movement charges the brain, they are also energizing the child's brain and allowing the energy to focus on the next more stationary activity.

A Ram Sam Sam (Music Together-Fiddle) .... Duple / Major

A Tisket-A Tasket (Music Copy) use with bean bags for balance: http://www.youtube.com/watch?v=67ZsPmQ-4dU .... Duple / Major

All Around the Kitchen (Music Copy): http://freesongsforkids.com/audios/all-around-kitchen see my sheet for things to do.. (See website)

All Around the Kitchen (Music Together-Maracas) .... Duple / Three classic blues forms of 12-bar, 8-bar, & 16-bar on A Minor

Allison's Camel (Music Copy) .... Duple / Major

Be-Ba-Butzeman (Music Copy) http://www.youtube.com/watch?v=JoMpflanAho in German .... Duple / Major

Betty Martin (Music Together-Tambourine) .... Duple / Major

Carnival of the Animals by Saint-Saens – use this recording to move like the animals titled in the musical sections (there are 13 different animals Saint-Seans' music depicts) .... (Use a classical music recording)

City Blues (Music Together-Bongos) CD#23 use with hoops .... Duple / Major

Crawdad (Music Together-Fiddle) .... Duple / Major

Drummers Marching (Music Together-Triangles) CD#23 .... Triple / Minor

Goin' To Boston (Music Together-Fiddle) perform with hoops ....Duple / Mixolydian on C

Hop Ol' Squirrel (Music Together-Maracas) .... Duple / Major

Hop Old Squirrel (Music Copy) do the motions of squirrel before adding instruments .... Duple / Major

Jumpin' Josie (Music Together-Maracas) .... Duple / Major

Ladybug (Music Together-Triangle) CD#17 movement improvisation .... Triple / Minor

Looby Loo (Music Copy) use with hoops .... Triple / Major

Merry-Go-Round (Music Together-Tambourine) use with scarves .... Triple / Minor

Monkey See, Monkey Do (Music Copy) travel movement .... Duple / Major

North Wind Doth Blow (Music Copy) scarves... Triple / Major

Old Betty Larkin (Music Copy) http://www.folklorist.org/song/Old_Betty_Larkin_(Betsy_Larkin,_You_Stole_My_Pard,_Steal_Partners,_Stole_My_Partner) .... Duple / Dorian on D

Paw Paw Patch (Music Together-Tambourine) hide and seek song & game .... Duple / Major

Riding In A Buggy (Music Copy) can use with hoops .... Duple / Major

See How I'm Jumping (Music Together-Bongos) CD#7 can use with hoops .... Duple / Minor

See the Pony Galloping (Music Together-Tambourine) use 2 scarves as reins for children as horses... Triple / Major

Teddy Bear, Teddy Bear (Music Copy) use with bean bags for balance – see music copy for ideas and tune .... Duple / Major

The Monkey Stomps travel movement .... Duple / Major

This 'n' That (Music Together-Tambourine) .... Duple / Mixolydian (quasi-Cuban)

This Train (Music Together-Drums) .... Duple / Dorian on D (Countermelodies)

Tingalayo (Music Together-Babies) movement or stick horses: www.youtube.com/watch?v=trCOfgwikjY .... Duple / Major

Train Is a-Comin'(Music Together-Bongos) CD#12 shakers..................... Duple / Major

Train To The City (Music Together-Maracas) make a train around the room .... Duple / Major

William Tell's Ride (Music Together-Maracas) ride with stick ponies .... Duple / Major & Minor

Wolf (We Are Dancing) (Music Copy) Dance with scarves .... Duple / Major

Steady Beat Activities Utilizing Instruments. (sticks, drums, shakers, jingles, scarves). Plan for 2-3 songs for the children to hear the steady beat and use instruments to match that beat. The song is introduced by singing first and using body percussion to illustrate the beats. Then these movements are transferred to playing steady beat instruments. The teacher always models the beats as the children simultaneously mirror. The children can use sticks in varying ways to keep the beat to a song with or without words. To encourage the "independent preschooler," the children can take turns thinking of various ways to keep the beat on the stick or drums, and the class can copy. Other instruments can be used to enhance a song after the song has been introduced by the teacher by singing and body percussion to illustrate the movements to come. Instruments can help to explore music concepts, such as, fast and slow, loud and quiet, and musical form (AB and ABA). Drums are wonderful instruments to use because children are able to play them with their hands, thereby developing a sensitivity of touch. This sensitivity of touch is a basic requirement for all instrument playing.

A Ram Sam Sam (Music Together-Fiddle) .... Duple / Major

Aiken Drum (Music Copy): http://www.youtube.com/watch?v=Vhi8CmTbuIo (drums) .... Duple / Major

Allee Galloo (Music Together-Triangles) CD#21 use scarves to beat & throw/catch .... Triple / Major

Apples and Cherries (Music Together-Fiddle) .... Duple / Major / Tonal Round

Baa, Baa Little Star (Music Together-Triangles) CD#20 sticks .... Duple / Major / Instrumental Play Along

Biddy Biddy (Music Together-Drums) shakers or jingles .... Duple / Major

Bim Bam (Music Together-Maracas) .... Duple / Minor

Bingo w/Orff (Mother Goose Club) instead of clapping they can play an Sol-Do bordun for the omitted letters) .... Duple / Major

Bongo Jam (Music Together-Bongo) CD#14 instrumental instrument jam .... Duple / Major / Instrumental Play Along

Bought Me A Cat (Music copy) Different Percussion Instrument Sounds .... Duple / Major

Breezes (Music Together-Triangles) CD#12 dance free style with scarves .... Triple / Mixolydian on D

By 'n' By (Music Together-Bells) jingles to count fingers/xylophones .... Duple / Major

Bye Baby Bunting Orff accompaniment .... Duple / Major

Canoe Song (Music Together-Bongos) CD#20 drums or sticks .... Duple / Minor

Charlie Over The Ocean w/Orff & game (Music Copy) .... Triple / Major

Chicken on the Fence Post (Music Copy) shakers /jingle sticks/drums .... Duple / Major

Clap Your Hands (Mother Goose Club) .... Duple / Major

Drummers Marching (Music Together-Triangles) CD#23 .... Triple / Minor

Dum Ditty Dum (Music Together-Flutes) different percussion instruments .... Duple / Major

Ensey, Weensey Spider (Music Together-Bongos) Orff- 5 note pentatonic pattern going up & down .... Triple (or Compound Duple) / Major

Five Fat Turkeys Are We (Music Copy) motions & drums .... Duple / Major

Five Little Monkeys (Music Copy) Orff & Drum with jingles-use with book as well .... Duple Rhythmic Chant

Frère Jacques (Music Together-Maracas) .... Duple / Major / Vocal and Instrumental Ostinatos

Grizzly Bear (loud and quiet sounding instruments) .... Duple / Major

Hickety Pickety My Black Hen (Music Copy) Orff .... Triple / Major

Hickory Dickory Dock (Music Copy) Drums & Orff.................................. Triple / Major

Hill and Gully Rider (Music Copy) drums/sticks or resonator bars .... Duple / Major

Hop Old Squirrel (Music Copy) Drum or Resonator Bars/Orff................. Duple / Major

I Had A Little Frog (Music Together-Flutes) guiros or drum ...... Duple Rhythmic Chant

I Had A Rooster (Music Copy) Different Percussion Instrument Sounds .... Triple / Major

I'm A Bell (Music Together-Maracas) .... Triple / Minor

I'm Hiding (Music Together-Triangles) rap with scarves .... Duple Rhythmic Chant

I've Been Working On The Railroad (Music Together-Flutes) (different percussion instruments) .... Duple / Major

I've Got The Rhythm In My Head (Music Together-Fiddle) .... Duple / Major

Isty Bitsy Spider (Music Copy) .... Triple / Major

Jack and Jill (Nursery Rhyme): http://www.youtube.com/watch?v=8RoAJqcn9E4 (bounce and Orff) (playing notes going up and then glissando down)
.... Triple / Major

Little Johnny Brown (Music Together-Bongos) CD#19 scarves
.... Duple / Natural Minor

Monkey See, Monkey Do (Music Copy) sticks .... Duple / Major

Naughty Kitty Cat (Music Copy) Drums/sticks or Resonator Bars/Orff
.... Duple / Major

Nothin' Blues (Music Together-Triangles) CD#2 steady beat with shakers or other percussion .... Duple / Major in Blues Style

Oh Dear! What Can The Matter Be? (Music Copy) scarves: http://www.youtube.com/watch?v=VNs6ey1Kb9U .... Triple / Major

Oh Mr. Sun (Music Copy): http://www.songsforteaching.com/folk/ohmrsun.php (triangles & shakers)... Duple / Major

Old McDonald Had A Farm (Music Copy) – use different percussion instruments for each animal .... Duple / Major

Pease Porridge Hot (Music Together-Maracas)........................ Duple Rhythmic Chant

Rain Song (Music Together-Triangles) CD#9- Orff or resonators for ostinato pattern & percussion instruments for rain storm .... Duple / Dorian on D

Rain Song (Music Together-Triangles) CD#9 sticks or drums .... Duple / Dorian on D

She'll Be Comin' 'Round The Mountain (Music Together-Bongos) use instruments for special effects .... Duple / Major

Sleep, Baby Sleep (Music Copy) Orff/Resonator Bars............................. Duple / Major

Somebody's Knocking At Your Door (Music Copy) use different words and drums: www.youtube.com/watch?v=y10DrAw549E .... Duple / Major

Ten Fingers (Music Together-Triangle) use jingles ....Duple Rhythmic Chant

The Frog In the Bog (Music Copy) guiros or drum or resonator bars ....Duple (with 2 triplets) / Major

The Snail and The Mouse (Music Together-Drums) ....Duple Rhythmic Chant

There's A Cobbler (Music Together-Drums) sticks ....Duple Rhythmic Chant

There's a Little Wheel-a-Turning (Music Together-Babies) .... Duple / Major

This Old Man (Music Together-Bongs) CD#8 different percussion instruments .... Duple / Major

This Train (Music Together-Drums) shakers .... Duple / Dorian on D (Countermelodies)

Three Little Kittens (Music Copy) Resonators... Triple / Major

Train Is a-Comin' (Music Together-Bongos) CD#12 shakers .... Duple / Major

Train To The City (Music Together-Maracas) shakers .... Duple / Major

Two Little Blackbirds (Music Copy) scarves or even shakers .... Duple / Major

Two Little Blackbirds (Music Together-Triangle) CD#26 shakers or jingles or scarves .... Duple / Major

Walking Through the Woods (Music Together-Bongos) CD#6 scarves .... Triple / Minor

Wee Willie Winkie (Nursery Rhyme) (Music Copy) Orff – see music copy for instructions .... Duple / Major

When Johnny Comes Marching Home .... Triple / Natural Minor

Who's That? (Music Together-Babies) scarves... Duple / Major

William, He Had Seven Songs (Music copy) Xylophones/shakers .... Duple / Minor

Music Stories / Story Songs / Sound Stories. (Orff xylophones / resonator bars). There are many reasons why stories and story songs are important in a music class, including the importance of language development and increased vocabulary. First, telling a story or creating a story through instruments is particularly important because it is an aural experience for the child. The children in class not only are allowed to listen to the story, but focus also on how the story would really sound if it were truly happening. The story becomes real through the imagination of creativity of the children and the instruments. This encourages good listening skills. Second, by telling or creating a story the child is asked to imagine. This is important as the child can be asked for the input in regards to instruments to add to the story or an imaginary journey to the farm or circus. This is important as the child progresses from concrete to abstract thought. Third, when telling or creating a story, the child can be asked for their input in regard to instruments to add to the story or an imaginary journey to the farm or circus. This gives the child ownership in the adventure and in turn grows confident independent thinking. Fourth, song stories provide opportunities for movement and vocal exploration. Children use their voices to imitate many things. For many children, it reinforces the difference between their singing and speaking voices. Regarding movement, even the roughest, toughest children are capable of moving expressively. It becomes very easy for them when they imagine themselves as someone or something else, such as a robin hopping across the lawn in search of a worm, or a sunflower growing tall.

**See Preschool Book List as well
**Great reference site: Preschooleducation.com and bethsmusicnotes.blogspot.com

Hickory Dickory Dock (song story with movement/hoops – music is sung while students are in hoop and when the clock strikes, they jump out and move around the hoops in the room to the steady beat of the song being played with variation. When the clock strikes again, they need to move into their hoop to sing the song again with the music. This repeats a couple of times and each time the music can get a little faster.)

Pop Goes the Wiesel (song with movement/hoops – music is played and children need to march around their hoop. Once a popping sound is played, they jump into the hoop and sing the song. When the pop is sung, they jump out of their hoop. A steady beat musical excerpt is played until the children hear the melody of "pop goes the weasel" and when they do the whole activity is repeated again.)

Dr. Foster (song story with movement/hoops – nursery rhyme is sung or recited with expression as children are in hoops and they finish with a big splash sound. The children jump out pretending to carry umbrellas and march to the steady beat of a song variation of rain sounds along with "it's raining, it's pouring" and when the "Dr. Foster" song or rhyme is heard again the children find their hoops and when the splash is played again, they jump inside to do the whole activity once more.)

Falling of the Leaves (Musical stories/pictures-Children will move to music that depicts sounds of leaves falling and swirling to the ground. The wind blows and more leaves come whirling and twirling to the ground. The wind blows stronger and the leaves blow form the ground back into the air and finally come to rest on the ground as the wind settles down. Movement can be done with scarves.)

Summer Sunflower Dance (Musical stories/pictures-Children will move to music that depicts Sunflower seeds rhythmically dropped into the soil and planted. The rain storm that waters the seeds and the sun that shines combine to help the seed grow. The sequence happens again and the Sunflower grows and grows. Then the weather changes, the wind blows and the sunflower droops to the ground. The bird fly and gather the seeds and the squirrels scamper to collect seed as well before running into the forest.)

Winter Fun (Musical stories/pictures-Children move to the music that depicts the children bundling up and running outside to the sparkling winter snow. They grab a handful of snow and squeeze it tight into a ball and roll it and roll it and roll it for the bottom portion of the snowman using lower notes. The sequence repeats 2 more times for the middle and the head of the snowman changing the pitch to make each level higher. Then staccato sounds to add the face before the children dance with their new friend.)

Spring Day at the Park (Musical stories/pictures-Children move to the music that depicts the children rhythmically walking to the park and enjoying some fun activities there such as the up and down sounds of the swings or the running up the stairs to slide down the slide. Then the fun day is interrupted by the sound of thunder as the rain starts to plop down at first and then much faster causing the children to stop and run home to the music of "It's raining, it's pouring".)

Tadpoles and Frogs (Musical story about things that change-Children will move to music that depicts a swimming tadpole that swims around and nibbles and then starts to grow and change. Grows legs and arms and wiggles it tail right off before it starts jumping around as a frog.)

Caterpillars and Butterflies (Musical story about things that change-Children move to music that depicts a crawling and nibbling caterpillar. The music then changes as the caterpillar crawls to the top of a leaf to start to change. Music changes as the musical suspense builds as the chrysalis is formed and finally cracks open to present a beautiful butterfly that needs to stretch its wings before it flies away.)

Dandelions and Blow Flowers (Musical story about things that change-Children move to music that depicts a dandelion seed that starts to grow and all the petals open to show its beautiful yellow flower and then the music changes as the flower closes up and all the yellow petals drop off. The suspense builds as the flower opens again as a blow flower and the wind blows to make the seed fly off in the wind carrying another dandelion seed.)

Flowering Seeds and Pumpkin Patch (Musical story about things that change-Children move to music that depicts a vine that grows along the ground. It opens into a beautiful flower but then the music changes as the flower wilts to reveal a little ball. The suspense grows as the ball grows into a big pumpkin that turns a bright orange in the sun. The story can continue to a popping sound as the pumpkin gets plucked from the pumpkin patch and scooped out to reveal a glowing face as it turns into a jack-o-lantern.)

Ananse and the Sticky Glue	Orff Sound Story
Three Billy Goats Gruff	Orff Sound Story
Doctor Foster	Triple / Major
Easter Bunny Story	Orff Sound Story
Five Little Monkeys (Music Copy) to be used with book of same title	Duple Rhythmic Chant
Goldilocks and the Three Bears	Sound Story
Grizzly Bear	Duple / Major
Hickory Dickory Dock	Triple / Major
Oliver Twist song story with movement/hoops	Triple / Major
Pop Goes the Weasel	Triple / Major
St. Nicholas Leaves a Gift	Orff Sound Story
Wee Willie Winkie song story with movement	Duple / Major

Rhythm and Tonal Patterns. Short and simple 2-4 beat rhythmic examples, both duple and triple meter patterns (quarter and eighth note rhythms) and 3-note easy solfége patterns (So-Mi-Do for major, Mi-Do-La for minor) are presented by the teacher and echoed by parents so toddlers can be bathed in rhythmic and tonal patterns taken both from their music and simply created. The teacher chants the neutral syllable "ba" for rhythm patterns, and sings the neutral syllable "bum" for tonal patterns. These patterns can be taken from the rhythm and tonal flash cards in Book 1A of the Knauss Music Curriculum. These patterns can also be taken from the songs just sung, or in the next song to be sung, to help establish tonality (major or minor) or rhythmic meter (duple or triple). These short patterns become the building blocks for children to later identify in music heard or sung, or even to create music of their own. Just like language is learned from words to phrases to sentences, so music is learned the same way; rhythmic and tonal patterns to phrases to creative songs. These patterns help develop a musical vocabulary, which also helps develop memory skills, an important focus skill for K-12 grades and beyond.

> Simple rhythm patterns of quarter and eighth notes on neutral syllable "ba"
> Complex rhythm patterns of any combinations on neutral syllable "ba"
> Duple and Triple rhythm patterns from Book 1A of Knauss Music Curriculum
> Simple tonal patterns of Do-Mi-So using neutral syllable "ba"
> Simple tonal patterns of La-Do-Mi using neutral syllable "ba"
> Tonal patterns from Book 1A of Knauss Music Curriculum

Focused Listening Activities. These songs are short examples of sounds of things or animals introduced in stories or songs. They quiet the child and settle the class, as well as teach the children to "listen actively" for whatever is pointed out. These activities help the children to focus their attention and quietly listen. They also help develop memory skills, help develop auditory clarity, as well as expand the child's vocabulary. The children can be asked to imitate each sound or describe it. Listening skills are developed. Researchers have concluded that good listening skills tends to having better grades in school.

> **When using the Orff instrument, establish a "listening position" and a "resting position" with the children when using the mallets and the instrument.

The Itsy-Bitsy Spider .... (Told and Illustrated by Iza Trapani)
(work with playing stepping notes that go up and down and glissandos)

Spider on the Floor (A Raffi Song to Read) .... (Illustrated by True Kelley)
(music is on back page - Jingles-shake them every time sing word "spider" and tap the body part to the steady beat as each part is sung)

May There Always Be Sunshine .... (Jim Gill)
(music is on front page - use open bordun D-A to keep steady beat. Make up their own favorite things to create their own story-illustrate at home and bring it back)

Dandelions Stars in the Grass ....(Mia Posada: Scholastic)
(as story is read use Orff instruments set up in a 5 note pentatonic pattern. Use instruments to create the image of flower growing by playing do through so together or so down through do when the root is burrowing down in the ground; as well as the flower opening up or flying in the wind by a glissando; when word "seed" is read they can tap on wood part of instrument.)

Butterflies .... (Karen Shapiro: Scholastic)
(use Orff instruments to create images as story is read...set up in an octave. Image of growing can be done by playing low "do" to high "do"; fluttering = glissando; as numbers are used to count, children can tap "do" same amount of times as numbers read. When they shed or pop their skin, children can tap on wood of instrument. Tap on big and smallest bars when talking about big and small. Skipped pg. 22-27)

The Jacket I Wear In The Snow .... (Shirley Neitzel)
(a repetitive layering book and as it is read and introduces another piece of winter clothing a child can use an instrument sound for each new item, being played only when their item is being read. Children can choose the instrument that represent their item of clothing.)

The Animal Boogie .... (Debbie Harter: Barefoot Books)
(music in the back of the book – use percussion instruments to create the sound for each of the animals introduced. They are to be played as that animal is introduced. On the chorus "shake, shake, boogie, woogie, oogie section" create a dance of shaking and rolling hands.)

Miss Mary Mack (Sing Along Stories)
....(Mary Ann Hoberman & Nadine Bernard Westcott)
(music is on front page and can be done as a singing, hand clapping song. Children can play whole song as a "do, re, mi, fa" song. The whole song can be sung using those 4 notes and as they sing it, they can play as well.)

There Were Ten In The Bed (Scholastic)
.... (Illustrated by Susan Chapman Calitri)
(music is on the back page. Children can play the "roll over" pattern of "so-mi-do" on their Orff instrument as the children sing it each time. Can also be used for solo opportunity by replacing the words "the little one said" with the name of a child... "then Mary said" and that child sings the "roll over" pattern and plays the "so-mi-do" pattern at the same time. Everyone sings the last "so-mi-do" pattern which is..."I found It" all-together.)

Five Little Monkeys Jumping on the Bed ....(Eileen Christelow)
(see Music Copy – Five Little Monkeys)

The Jazz Fly .... (Matthew Gollub)
(CD included with book...Talk about instruments used in a jazz quartet. Read story and use different percussion instruments for the fly and the animals that the fly asks for directions. Play and improvise all instruments together as the jazz music plays on the CD at the end.)

Over in the Garden ....(Jennifer Ward)
(music is in the book. Use different percussion sound for each animal introduced in the book. Can use Orff instruments for each bug as well...crawling & marching = alternating do-mi-broken bordun pattern; buzzing or flying = glissando patterns; jumping = do-mi hands together-open bordun pattern. Or creatively make up own patterns for the actions of the bugs on the Orff instruments.)

Tadpoles .... (Betsy James: Scholastic)
(Creatively add sounds on Orff instruments to help bring the story to life as if it were actually happening. Use patterns such as climbing up the pentatonic scale to depict growing of both little Davey and the tadpoles. Playing 2 notes hands together for jumping. Play descending pentatonic scale for falling. Glissando for sound of tadpoles swimming...etc. Read the story expressively as well.)

Joseph Had a Little Overcoat .... (Simms Taback)
(music is on the back page. Can use Orff for I and V chords do-so to accompany the song and on the "la's" use triangles or shakers to accompany the singing in that section.)

Peter and the Wolf .... (Retold and Illustrated by Michele Lemieux)
Read story and have short sound clips to illustrate the character sounds. As they play, flashcards can be shown of the animal with the instrument that is played. You can also have children move as the different characters such as scarves to fly high like the bird or scarves to wiggle low as a swimming duck or drums to march around like hunter as well as sticks used put on shoulder and rubbed like playing violin for Peter etc....when the sound and character s are done the children freeze and sit back down for the story again.

The Journey Home from Grandpa's.. (Jemima Lumley)
(musical story-CD included with book...children can choose a different percussion sound to make the sound for the vehicle that they are chosen for in the story. They play their sound effect as their vehicle is being sung.)

We All Go Traveling By ....(Sheena Roberts)
(musical story-CD included with book...use a different percussion instrument to depict the sounds for the different ways to travel. This story is cumulative so the instruments repeatedly add on but continue to play as each new instrument is introduced through a new way to travel)

Walking Through The Jungle..(Debbie Harter)
(musical story-CD included with book...can use different percussion instruments to play for each new animal the child discovers. Also Orff can be used to play the song using 5 notes C-G. Do not modulate in the higher key. Children echo the pattern by singing and playing it right after the teacher...last line all do together "chasing after me"-so-fa-mi-re-do)

We're Going On A Bear Hunt.. (Michael Rosen)
(use different percussion instruments to create the sound of each activity the children go through to get to the cave. For example: guiros = stumble/trip forest, and cabasa = squishy mud, etc. Can use body percussion to march on lap to get to each new location while chanting the repetitive section or even put the marching ostinato with the chant on Orff instruments to do a broken bordun.)

There Was An Old Lady Who Swallowed A Fly .... (Simms Taback)
(tune: http://www.youtube.com/watch?v=xa1j680x5Fk)
(story can be sung with the tune above and again each new animal or bug can be played on a different percussion instrument as it is being sung. It is an accumulative story so each new bug or animal is added to the sounds already played.)

There Was A Shy Fellow Who Swallowed A Cello
.... (Barbara S. Garriel, John O'Brien)
(same concept as above...as the new instrument is being swallowed you can have a very short excerpt to play of that particular instrument sound.)

Pete The Cat (I love my white shoes) .... (Eric Litwin)
(for free song go to: http://www.harpercollins.com/childrens/feature/petethecat Use resonator bars to accompany children as they sing.)

Pete The Cat And His 4 Groovy Buttons .... (Eric Litwin)
(for free song go to: http://www.harpercollins.com/childrens/feature/petethecat ...use resonator bars to accompany children as they sing. Can be 2 groups that are directed to play: group 1 plays C-E-G; group 2 plays F-A)

The Wheels On The Bus .... (Raffi)
(use percussion instruments for the sound effects)

The Mitten .... (Jan Brett)
(After each new animal snuggles into the mitten; children sing to the tune of "Farmer in the Dell"..."there's a (rabbit-new animal) in the mitten, (a rabbit) in the mitten, Reigh-Ro the Rerry-o, a (rabbit) in the mitten". The first sound "R" for rabbit is the sound used in "Heigh-Ho the Merry-o." Great with language development. Children sing that section and discover the new animal and the first letter sound of that animal to use as they sing the next verse. Children can also use different percussion instruments when they sing about each new animal that snuggles into the mitten.)

What's This? .... (Caroline Mockford)
(Use Orff instruments to create the imagery of the story coming to life...on the words "What's This", tap Do then So notes in a key of your choosing. For "grow" play 5 notes Do-So. For "seed" hit "Do". For the words "fly or taller" glissando going up. For "water" hit any notes like sprinkling water. For "hop" tap any 2 notes together as if hopping on the instrument. Look for good instrument technique as children play.)

Baby Beluga (A Raffi Song to Read) .... (Ashley Wolff)
(Have 3 ensemble groups ready to tap steady beat on the instruments set up with these particular chords: Group 1 "C" chord; group 2 "G chord"; group 3 "F chord"; teacher can have the "D chord". Children sing the story and play on the chorus.)

From Head To Toe .... (Eric Carle)
   (add rhythm or tune. Can read the story and have children use percussion instruments to answer the rhythm question that the teacher makes up. Teacher can sing the story by making up a tune using mi-so-la-notes where they ask the question if the children can do it…for example "so-mi-so-mi-so-la-so…mi-mi-so-la" and have children answer "la-la-so-mi" along with doing the same motions that they are asked to do.

Brown Bear, Brown Bear What Do You See.. (Eric Carle)
   (for Orff instruments there can be 2 groups of children: 1 group asking the question and 1 group answering. It can also be set up with the teacher being the question and the children answering. Sing and play the story using so-mi notes (so-mi-so-mi-so-mi-so) on question part and on the answer section use so mi do notes (so-mi-so-mi-so-mi-do)

Polar Bear, Polar Bear, What do You Hear?.. (Eric Carle)
   (Can read the story and use percussion instruments be the sounds of the animals making the noise on each page. Children can choose the instrument that best makes the sound to represent the animal sound that they were chosen to represent.)

Ananse and the Sticky Glue
   .... (Christi Cari Miller & Hal Leonard: Orff Sound Story)
   (Music copy-use teaching instructions given or create your own to add sound effects to the story)

Lion And The Mouse .... (Sound Story)
   (Children can decide by listening what percussion instrument can make a low sound and which makes a high sound when presented with different sound choices. Tell the story of the Lion and the mouse and each child can have a percussion instrument that they decided makes a high sound for the mouse and a low sound for the lion. As the teacher reads "the lion" the low instruments is played and conducted to stop. The same is done for the mouse and the high sound.)

The Tortoise and the Hare .... (Sound Story)
   (Children can play a shaker and tap fast for the Hare and can use a drum to play very slowly for the Tortoise as his named is called. The entrance and stopping point can be conducted by the teacher along with practicing resting position for when the story is recited without sound effects.)

Three Billy Goats Gruff .... (Orff Sound Story)
   (Music copy-use teaching instructions given or create your own to add sound effects to the story. Make sure to use different sized Orff instruments for low, medium and high sounds for the different sized goats or percussion sounds if using those type of instruments to bring the story to life)

Goldilocks and The Three Bears .... (Sound Story)
   (Read or recite the story and use instruments that have low, medium, and high pitches. Can use different choices of sounds and have the children pick which sound is the highest or lowest. Keep the instrument sounds from the same family of instruments such as ringing sounds or wood sounds. The instruments are used as Goldilocks tries the different sizes of bowls, chairs, beds, and bears. Goldilocks can also have her own sound. *I also have a song –see Music Copy- Goldilocks Song- where the story can be sung and Orff instruments can accompany by playing Do-So in the key together as an open bordun. Orff Instruments can also play that open bordun on the big, medium, and tiny items using 3 different pitched Orff instruments. Again try to keep the sound the same using all xylophones – soprano, alto, and bass or all glockenspiels or all metallophones.

The Little Old Lady Who Was Not Afraid Of Anything ....(Linda Williams)
   (Halloween. Story is read and the sound effects are added first with the body percussion already told through the story. The next time story is read instruments can be used to be the sounds of the shoes clomping and shirt shaking and pants wiggling as well as pumpkin shouting Boo which is great on the flexatone instrument.)

10 Fat Turkeys (Thanksgiving) .... (Tony Johnston)
   (Story can be read and do motions for "Gobble gobble wibble wobble whoops" section of the song and use percussion instruments for the different turkeys. Can also read the story and on the "Gobble gobble wibble wobble whoops" section the Orff instruments can play a C scale going up or down for every syllable and sing it and on the "oops" which changes each time the children can play a glissando.)

The First Day Of Winter (Christmas) ....(Denise Fleming)
   (Story can be sung to the tune of "The 12 Days of Christmas" and each day of Christmas when a new item has been given a new percussion sound can be added for that item. Another idea is that each time a new item has been given an added child plays the open bordun (do & so) in the key of the song

St. Nicholas Leaves A Gift (Christmas) ....(Orff Sound Story)
   (Music copy-use teaching instructions given or create your own to add sound effects to the story)

Pete The Cat Saves Christmas.. (Eric Litwin)
   (read the story with much expression and when the singing section comes children can use Orff instruments of choir bells in groups of chords. (I, IV, and V) in the key of the song. Children play their notes when directed by the teacher to the steady beat. An example of this story being read and the song in the story go to http://www.youtube.com/watch?v=a6Qiiksp4sg)

Easter Bunny Story (Easter) ....(Orff Sound Story)
   (Music copy-use teaching instructions given or create your own to add sound effects to the story)

Preschoolers Music Together Books Index

The Music Together Books included in this index are:

Music Together: Tambourine Song Collection
Music Together: Fiddle Song Collection
Music Together: Triangle Song Collection
Music Together: Drum Song Collection
Music Together: Bongos Song Collection
Music Together: Maracas Song Collection
Music Together: Bells Song Collection
Music Together: Sticks Song Collection
Music Together: Flute Song Collection
Music Together: Summer Songs 1
Music Together: Summer Songs 2
Music Together: Summer Songs 3
Music Together: Babies
Music Together: Family Favorites Songbook for Teachers

Music Together: Tambourine Song Collection

Guilmartin, K.K. & Levinowitz, L.M. (2004, 2007). *Music together: Tambourine song collection*. Princeton, NJ: Music Together LLC. www.musictogether.com. (CD, 2007). CD#: MTTA13-CD.

Contents

Betty Martin (Traditional)	p. 19	Duple / Major
Cradle Song (W. Blake & K. Guilmartin)	p. 29	Duple / Major
Ding Dong, Ding Dong (Traditional)	p. 41	Duple / Major / Tonal Round
Good News (Traditional African American Spiritual)	p. 45	Duple / Major
Goodbye, So Long, Farewell (K. Guilmartin)	p. 47	Triple / Major
Green and Blue (K. Guilmartin)	p. 22	Triple Rhythmic Chant
Hello Song (K. Guilmartin)	p. 13	Duple / Major
Hey Ya Na (Traditional Native American Apache)	p. 23	Duple / Natural Minor or Dorian
Hippity, Happity, Hoppity (Doug Morris)	p. 36	Triple Rhythmic Chant
Merry-Go Round (Lynn Lobban)	p. 39	Triple / Minor
Old Brass Wagon (Traditional)	p. 15	Duple / Major

One Little Owl (Traditional) .... p. 21	Duple / Minor
Pawpaw Patch (Traditional)... p. 37	Duple / Major
Raisins and Almonds (Traditional) .... p. 46	Triple / Minor
Ride-O (Traditional) .... p. 16	Duple / Major
Round Robin (Rebecca Frezza) .... p. 17	Duple / Major / Tonal Round
Scarborough Fair (Traditional)..................................... p. 43	Triple / Minor
Secrets (K. Guilmartin, L. Levinowitz, & Linda Betlejeski) .... p. 40	Duple Rhythmic Chant
See the Pony Galloping (Traditional) .... p. 24	Triple / Major
Sneakin' 'Round the Room (K. Guilmartin)............... p. 35	Duple / Minor (can be varied or Triple)
Tambourine Jam (K. Guilmartin)................................ p. 30	Duple / Major / Instrument Play Along with Minor contrasting section
This 'N' That (K. Guilmartin) .... p. 42	Duple / Mixolydian (quasi-Cuban)
Tingalayo (Traditional Spanish) .... p. 18	Duple / Major
Tricks With Sticks (K. Guilmartin) .... p. 26	Duple Rhythmic Chant / Major Tonality in other sections
Wedding Dance (Traditional).................................... p. 25	Duple / Major with lowered 2nd, 6th, and 7th (Middle Eastern)

Music Together: Fiddle Song Collection

Guilmartin, K.K. & Levinowitz, L.M. (2006, 2009). *Music together: Fiddle song collection*. Princeton, NJ: Music Together LLC. www.musictogether.com. (CD, 2003). CD#: MTFI09-CD.

Contents

A Ram Sam Sam (Traditional) .... p. 19	Duple / Major
Apples and Cherries (Traditional) .... p. 17	Duple / Major / Tonal Round
Bela Boya (Traditional Bulgarian Folksong) .... p. 25	Unusual Meter (7/8) / Implied Dorian Tonality
Butterfly (L. Levinowitz)... p. 40	Triple / Dorian on B
Can You Do This? (K. Guilmartin & L. Levinowitz)..... .... p. 24	Duple / Lydian on C
Crawdad (Traditional).. p. 15	Duple / Major
Goin' To Boston (Traditional American Folksong) .... p. 23	Duple / Mixolydian on C
Goodbye, So Long, Farewell (K. Guilmartin)............. p. 46	Triple / Major

Hello Song (K. Guilmartin) .... p. 13   Duple / Major
Here Is the Beehive (Traditional)................................ p. 33   Triple Rhythmic Chant
Hiné Ma Tov (Traditional Israeli Folksong) .... p. 37   Duple / Dorian on E
I've Got The Rhythm In My Head (American Singing Game)
.... p. 36   Duple / Major
Lauren's Waltz (K. Guilmartin)..................................... p. 29   Triple / Mixolydian on G
    (Middle section C Major / Instrumental Play Along)
Los Fandangos (Traditional Spanish Folksong) .... p. 22   Triple / Minor
Marching and Drumming (American Civil War Melody)
.... p. 35   Triple / Natural Minor
Mississippi Cats (K. Guilmartin) .... p. 41   Duple Rhythmic Chant
No More Pie (Traditional) .... p. 39   Duple / Minor Blues
Old King Cole (K. Guilmartin) .... p. 21   Duple / Natural Minor
Shady Grove (Traditional)... p. 28   Duple / Re Pentatonic based on C
Shenandoah (Traditional American Folksong).......... p. 45   Duple / Major
Singin' Every Day (K. Guilmartin, South African Melody)
.... p. 43   Duple / Major
Sweet Potato (Traditional Afro-American Folksong)
.... p. 27   Duple / Major
The Sounds Of Fall (K. Guilmartin)............................. p. 16   Duple Rhythmic Chant
This Little Light Of Mine (Traditional)....................... p. 44   Duple / Major
Walking Song (K. Guilmartin).................................... p. 18   Duple / Mixolydian on D

Music Together: Triangle Song Collection

Guilmartin, K.K. & Levinowitz, L.M. (2003, 2006). *Music together: Triangle song collection*. Princeton, NJ: Music Together LLC. www.musictogether.com. (CD, 2006). CD#: MTTR12-CD.

Contents

Allee Galloo (Traditional).. p. 45   Triple / Major
Ally Bally (Traditional)... p. 29   Duple / Major
Baa, Baa, Little Star (K. Guilmartin) .... p. 30   Duple / Major / Instrumental Play Along
Bird Song (Doug Morris) .... p. 39   Triple / Phrygian on C
Breezes (K. Guilmartin)... p. 35   Triple / Mixolydian on D
Camels (K. Guilmartin).. p. 25   Duple / Implied Major with lowered 2nd
Can You Do What I Do? (Traditional)........................ p. 21   Duple Rhythmic Chant
Dance with Me (Traditional)....................................... p. 14   Duple & Triple / Major
Drummers Marching (Linda Jessup) .... p. 42   Triple / Minor

Goodbye, So Long, Farewell (K. Guilmartin)	p. 47	Triple / Major
Hello Song (K. Guilmartin)	p. 13	Duple / Major
Hey, Ho, Nobody Home (Traditional)	p. 28	Duple (Swing Rhythm) / Minor
I'm Hiding (K. Guilmartin)	p. 37	Duple Rhythmic Chant
Ladybug (Lynn Lobban)	p. 19	Triple / Dorian Implied
Mariá Isabel (Traditional Spanish Folksong)	p. 27	Duple / Major
Nothin' Blues (K. Guilmartin & J.C. Lewis)	p. 18	Duple / Major in Blues Style
Old Blue (Traditional)	p. 38	Duple / Mixolydian on D
Rain Song (K. Guilmartin)	p. 20	Duple / Dorian on D
Rolling a Round Ball (Sally Weaver)	p. 24	Triple / Dorian on C
Skip to My Lou (Traditional)	p. 41	Duple / Major
Stick Dance (K. Guilmartin)	p. 43	Unusual Meter (5/4) / Various Implied Tonalities (Lydian) and some Blues
Ten Fingers (Traditional)	p. 17	Duple Rhythmic Chant
The Train Song (Art Levinowitz)	p. 15	Duple / Major (Vocal Harmony Parts)
The Water is Wide (Traditional)	p. 46	Duple / Major
Two Little Blackbirds (K. Guilmartin)	p. 23	Duple / Major

Music Together: Drum Song Collection

Guilmartin, K.K. & Levinowitz, L.M. (2007, 2010). *Music together: Drum song collection*. Princeton, NJ: Music Together LLC. www.musictogether.com. (CD, 2012). CD#: MTDR13-CD.

Contents

Arirang (Traditional Korean Folksong)	p. 44	Triple / Do Pentatonic on G with accidental Bb)
Biddy Biddy (Traditional)	p. 14	Duple / Major
Clap Your Hands (Traditional)	p. 15	Duple / Mixolydian on D
Drum and Sing (K. Guilmartin)	p. 41	Duple / Minor
Duérmete Niño Bonito (Traditional Spanish Folksong)	p. 29	Triple / Minor
Everybody Loves Saturday Night (Traditional)	p. 45	Duple / Major
Goodbye, So Long, Farewell (K. Guilmartin)	p. 47	Triple / Major
Hello Song (K. Guilmartin)	p. 13	Duple / Major
John the Rabbit (Traditional)	p. 17	Duple / Major
Kookaburra (Traditional)	p. 43	Duple / Major
My Ball (L. Levinowitz)	p. 25	Unusual Meter (7/8) Rhythmic Chant

Play Along (K. Guilmartin)	p. 30	Duple / Major / Instrumental Play Along
Playin' in the Kitchen (K. Guilmartin)	p. 39	Duple Rhythmic Chant and Major Tonal Singing
Pussycat (J. Kuhns)	p. 23	Mixed Triple / Phrygian on E
Rig-A-Jig-Jig (Traditional)	p. 40	Triple / Major
Roll Over (Traditional)	p. 21	Duple / Major
Sailing Song (L. Levinowitz)	p. 26	Triple / Mixolydian on D
She Sells Sea Shells (K. Guilmartin)	p. 19	Duple / Implied Dorian on D
Sneak and Peak (L. Levinowitz)	p. 20	Duple / Dorian on D
The Snail and the Mouse (Traditional)	p. 18	Duple Rhythmic Chant
There's a Cobbler (Traditional)	p. 33	Duple Rhythmic Chant
They Come Back (K. Guilmartin)	p. 35	Duple / Major
This Train (Traditional)	p. 27	Duple / Dorian on D Countermelodies)
Ticking and Tocking (K. Guilmartin & L. Levinowitz)	p. 24	Triple / Lydian on F
Tomorrow's Now Today (K. Guilmartin & L. Guilmartin)	p. 46	Duple / Major

Music Together: Bongos Song Collection

Guilmartin, K.K. & Levinowitz, L.M. (2008). *Music together: Bongos song collection*. Princeton, NJ: Music Together LLC. www.musictogether.com. (CD, 2005). CD#: MTBO11-CD.

Contents

Bongo Jam (K. Guilmartin)	p. 28	Duple / Major / Instrumental Play Along
Canoe Song (Traditional)	p. 39	Duple / Minor
City Blues (K. Guilmartin)	p. 45	Duple / Major
Ding-A-Ding (K. Guilmartin)	p. 24	Duple / Dorian / Combinable
Down Under (K. Guilmartin)	p. 43	Unusual Paired (6/8 & 4/4)
Eensy, Weensy Spider (Traditional American)	p. 33	Triple (or Compound Duple) / Major
Every Day (K. Guilmartin)	p. 15	Combined (Duple with Triplets) / Rhythm Activity
Fireworks (L. Levinowitz)	p. 22	Triple / Rhythm Round
Goodbye, So Long, Farewell (K. Guilmartin)	p. 47	Triple / Major
Greensleeves (Traditional English)	p. 36	Triple / Harmonic Minor

Hello Song (K. Guilmartin) .... p. 13	Duple / Major
Hey, Diddle, Diddle (K. Guilmartin)........................ p. 17	Duple / Minor
Li'L 'Liza Jane / Funga Alafia (Traditional Afro-American)	
.... p. 40	Duple / Major / Partner Songs
Little Johnny Brown (Traditional Afro-American)..... p. 37	Duple / Natural Minor
Mountain Dew (Traditional Irish) .... p. 34	Triple (or Compound Duple) / Major
My Bonnie (H. J. Fulmer) .... p. 46	Triple / Major
Open and Shut Them (Traditional Flemish).............. p. 16	Duple / Major
Palo, Palo (Traditional Dominican Republic) .... p. 23	Duple / Major
See How I'm Jumping (Traditional Flemish) .... p. 20	Duple / Minor
She'll Be Comin' 'Round the Mountain (Traditional American)	
.... p. 14	Duple / Major
Shoo, Fly, Don't Bother Me (Frank Campbell & Billy Reeves)	
.... p. 35	Duple / Major
Sleepyhead (Lyn Ransom)....................................... p. 27	Duple / Major
This Old Man (Traditional) .... p. 21	Duple / Major
Train is a-Comin' (Traditional Afro-American).......... p. 25	Duple / Major
Walking Through the Woods (K. Guilmartin)........... p. 19	Triple / Minor

Music Together: Maracas Song Collection

Guilmartin, K.K. & Levinowitz, L.M. (2005, 2008). *Music together: Maracas song collection*. Princeton, NJ: Music Together LLC. www.musictogether.com.

Contents

All Around The Kitchen (Traditional) .... p. 18	Duple / Three classic blues forms of 12-bar, 8-bar, & 16-bar on A Minor
Bim Bam (Traditional).. p. 22	Duple / Minor
Brincan Y Bailan (Traditional) .... p. 36	Duple / Minor
Cloud Song (Linda Jessup)....................................... p. 41	Triple / Minor
Dancing With Teddy (K. Guilmartin) .... p. 35	Triple / Major
Dee Da Dum (K. Guilmartin) .... p. 37	Duple / Major / Jazz Style
Doodle (L. Levinowitz) .... p. 27	Duple (Swing) / Dorian on D
Five Little Mice (Traditional).................................... p. 33	Duple Rhythmic Chant
Frère Jacques (Traditional) .... p. 44	Duple / Major / Vocal and Instrumental Ostinatos
Goin' For Coffee (K. Guilmartin) .... p. 30	Duple / Blues on C / Instrumental Play Along
Goodbye, So Long, Farwell (K. Guilmartin).............. p. 46	Triple / Major
Hello Song (K. Guilmartin) .... p. 13	Duple / Major

Hop Ol' Squirrel (Traditional)	p. 25	Duple / Major
I'm A Bell (L. Levinowitz)	p. 23	Triple / Minor
Jack Be Nimble (K. Guilmartin)	p. 40	Triple Rhythmic Chant
Jumpin' Josie (Traditional)	p. 14	Duple / Do Pentatonic on D
Pease Porridge Hot (Traditional)	p. 15	Duple Rhythmic Chant
Play the Drum (K. Guilmartin)	p. 43	Duple / Major
Russian Folk Song (Traditional)	p. 45	Duple / Major
Su La Li (Bonnie Light)	p. 29	Duple / Minor
The Sad Little Puppy (K. Guilmartin)	p. 39	Duple / Minor
Train To the City (Traditional)	p. 28	Duple / Major
Tsakonikos (Traditional)	p. 26	Unusual Meter (5/4) / Natural Minor
Wiggle! (L. Levinowitz)	p. 17	Duple / Major
William Tell's Ride (Rossini, arr. L. Ransom & K. Guilmartin)	p. 21	Duple / Major and Minor

Music Together: Bells Song Collection

Guilmartin, K.K. & Levinowitz, L.M. (2009). *Music together: Bells song collection*. Princeton, NJ: Music Together LLC. www.musictogether.com.

Contents

Brahms' Lullaby (Johannes Brahms)	p. 44	Triple / Major
By 'n' By (Traditional)	p. 29	Duple / Major
Celebration Song (Traditional Hasidic)	p. 23	Duple / Israeli Scale (Major with lowered 2nd)
De Colores (Traditional Mexican)	p. 27	Triple / Major
Deedle Dumpling (Chris Posluszny)	p. 25	Duple / Dorian
Foolin' Around (K. Guilmartin)	p. 30	Duple / Minor & Major / Instrumental
French Folk Song (Traditional French)	p. 37	Duple / Major
French Folk Song [Teacher Mixes] (on CD)		
Goodbye, So Long, Farewell (K. Guilmartin)	p. 45	Triple / Major
Hello Song (K. Guilmartin)	p. 13	Duple / Major
Hopping and Sliding (K. Guilmartin)	p. 18	Usual Paired (2/4 & 3/4) / Minor & Major
I'm Gonna Play Today (Traditional American)	p. 14	Duple / Major
Lukey's Boat (Traditional)	p. 26	Duple / Major
Me, You, and We (K. Guilmartin)	p. 36	Duple / Major
Misty Morning (K. Guilmartin)	p. 39	Triple / Minor (D Dorian & Natural)
Mr. Rabbit (Traditional)	p. 43	Duple / Major
My Lady Wind (K. Guilmartin)	p. 19	Duple / Major

Obwisana (Traditional Ghana)	p. 21	Duple / Major
Rhythms and Rhymes [Teacher Mixes] (on CD)		
Rhythms and Rhymes	p. 15	Duple Rhythm Chant
Robby Roly (K. Guilmartin)	p. 38	Duple / Minor
Robby Roly [Teacher Mixes] (on CD)		
Snowflakes (L. Levinowitz)	p. 22	Unusual (5/8) / Rhythmic Chant
Splishing and Splashing (K. Guilmartin)	p. 35	Duple with Triplets / Rhythmic Chant
The Bells of Westminster (Traditional)	p. 42	Duple / Major / Round & Countermelodies
The Bells of Westminster [Teacher Mixes] (on CD)		
Trot, Old Joe (Traditional)	p. 41	Duple / Major
Two Little Kitty Cats (Traditional)	p. 17	Duple / Minor
Who's That? (Traditional)	p. 33	Duple / Major

Music Together: Sticks Song Collection

Guilmartin, K.K. & Levinowitz, L.M. (2010). *Music together: Sticks song collection*. Princeton, NJ: Music Together LLC. www.musictogether.com. (CD, 2007). CD#: MTST11-CD.

Contents

Blow the Wind Southerly (Traditional)	p. 37	Triple / Major
Don Alfredo Baila (Traditional Catalonian)	p. 39	Duple / Major
Follow Me Down to Carlow (Traditional)	p. 17	Triple / Minor (or Dorian)
Goodbye, So Long, Farewell (K. Guilmartin)	p. 45	Triple / Major
Great Big Stars (Traditional Appalachian)		Duple / Major
Happy Puppy, Silly Cat (Sally Weaver)	p. 22	Unusual (7/8) / Major
Hello Song (K. Guilmartin)	p. 13	Duple / Major
Husha My Baby (Traditional South African)		Duple / Minor
I'm Freezing! (K. Guilmartin)	p. 24	Duple Chant
Jack-In-The-Box (Traditional)	p. 35	Triple / Rhythm Chant
Mary Wore a Red Dress (Traditional)	p. 18	Duple / Major
May All Children (K. Guilmartin)	p. 44	Multi-Metric (2/4, 3/4, 4/4) / Major
Mix It Up! (K. Guilmartin)	p. 38	Duple / G Mixolydian
Nigun (Traditional)	p. 25	Duple / Minor
Play Along, Too (K. Guilmartin)	p. 31	Duple / Major / Instrumental
Pop! Goes the Weasel (Traditional)	p. 28	Compound Triple (6/8) / Major
Ridin' in the Car (K. Guilmartin)	p. 15	Duple / Major

Roll That Little Ball (Traditional) .... p. 27   Duple / Major
Spin and Stop (L. Levinowitz).................................... p. 19   Triple Minor
Stick Tune (K. Guilmartin)... p. 21   Duple / D Mixolydian
The Love Song of Kangding (Traditional Sichuan Chinese)
....   Duple / Minor
The Tailor and the Mouse (Traditional).................... p. 36   Duple / Minor
Trot to Grandma's House (Traditional) .... p. 41   Duple / Major
Water Play (K. Guilmartin)..   Triple Rhythm Activity
When the Saints Go Marching In (Traditional) .... p. 43   Duple / Major

Music Together: Flute Song Collection

Guilmartin, K.K. & Levinowitz, L.M. (2010). *Music together: Flute song collection.* Princeton, NJ: Music Together LLC. www.musictogether.com.

Contents

Aeolian Dance (K. Guilmartin)	p. 21	Duple / Aeolian / Sung Neutral Syllable & Danced
All the Pretty Little Horses (Traditional)	p. 45	Duple / Minor (Aeolian or Natural)
Dance to Your Daddy (Traditional)	p. 35	Triple / Minor
Dum Ditty Dum (Traditional)	p. 18	Duple / Major
Goodbye, So Long, Farewell (K. Guilmartin)	p. 46	Triple / Major
Harvest Dance (K. Guilmartin & L. Levinowitz)	p. 40	Triple / Major / Sung Neutral Syllable & Danced
Hello Song (K. Guilmartin)	p. 13	Duple / Major
Hey Lolly, Lolly (Traditional)	p. 14	Duple / Major
I Had a Little Frog (Traditional)	p. 15	Duple Rhythm Chant
I've Been Working on the Railroad (Traditional)	p. 43	Duple / Major
Jim Along Josie (Traditional)	p. 33	Duple / Major
Leaves Are Falling (Rebecca Frezza)	p. 27	Duple / Dorian on E / Round
Ran Tin Tinnah (Traditional Celtic)	p. 25	Duple / Major
Rocketship (Rebecca Frezza)	p. 36	Unusual (5/4) / Rhythmic Chant
Sandpiper (K. Guilmartin)	p. 20	Duple / Major
Saying and Doing (K. Guilmartin)	p. 23	Triple Rhythmic Chant
Shake Those 'Simmons Down (Traditional)	p. 28	Duple / Major
Simple Gifts (Traditional)	p. 30	Duple / Major / Instrumental Play Along
The Crow Song (Traditional)	p. 37	Duple / Major / Sung Neutral Syllable
The Earth is Our Mother (Traditional)	p. 19	Duple / Minor
The Riddle Song (Traditional)	p. 29	Duple / Major
The Three Ravens (Traditional)	p. 17	Duple / Minor
There's a Little Wheel a-Turnin' (Traditional)	p. 24	Duple / Major
Tum Balalaika (Traditional)	p. 41	Triple / Minor
Vengan a Ver (Traditional Argentinian)	p. 39	Duple / Major

Music Together: Summer Songs 1

Guilmartin, K.K. & Levinowitz, L.M. (2001). *Music together: Summer songs 1*. Princeton, NJ: Music Together LLC. www.musictogether.com.

Contents

Song	Page	Description
A Ram Sam Sam (Traditional)	p. 20	Duple / Major
Deedle Dumpling (Chris Posluszny)	p. 33	Duple / Dorian
Goodbye, So Long, Farewell (K. Guilmartin)	p. 39	Triple / Major
Happy Puppy, Silly Cat (Sally Weaver)	p. 27	Unusual (7/8) / Major
Hello Song (K. Guilmartin)	p. 11	Duple / Major
Here Is the Beehive (Traditional)	p. 13	Triple Rhythmic Chant
Hey, Diddle, Diddle (K. Guilmartin)	p. 12	Duple / Minor
Hiné Ma Tov (Traditional Israeli Folksong)	p. 16	Duple / Dorian on E
I've Got The Rhythm In My Head (American Singing Game)	p. 17	Duple / Major
Jim Along Josie (Traditional)	p. 35	Duple / Major
Mariá Isabel (Traditional Spanish Folksong)	p. 37	Duple / Major
My Bonnie (H. J. Fulmer)	p. 38	Triple / Major
My Lady Wind (K. Guilmartin)	p. 21	Duple / Major
Play Along (K. Guilmartin)	p. 25	Duple / Major / Instrumental Play Along
Play the Drum (K. Guilmartin)	p. 15	Duple / Major
Rolling a Round Ball (Sally Weaver)	p. 30	Triple / Dorian on C
Ten Fingers (Traditional)	p. 19	Duple Rhythmic Chant
The Two Birds (Mother Goose)	p. 31	Duple Rhythm Chant with Triplets
Tomorrow's Now Today (K. Guilmartin & L. Guilmartin)	p. 24	Duple / Major
Tricks With Sticks (K. Guilmartin)	p. 22	Duple Rhythmic Chant / Major Tonality in other sections
Two Little Kitty Cats (Traditional)	p. 29	Duple / Minor

Music Together: Summer Songs 2

Guilmartin, K.K. & Levinowitz, L.M. (2007). *Music together: Summer songs 2*. Princeton, NJ: Music Together LLC. www.musictogether.com.

Contents

Song	Page	Description
Allee Galloo (Traditional)	p. 37	Triple / Major
Butterfly (L. Levinowitz)	p. 36	Triple / Dorian on B
Crawdad (Traditional)	p. 15	Duple / Major
Doodle (L. Levinowitz)	p. 33	Duple (Swing) / Dorian on D
Eensy, Weensy Spider (Traditional American)	p. 18	Triple (or Compound Duple) / Major
Fireworks (L. Levinowitz)	p. 19	Triple Rhythmic Chant
Five Little Mice (Traditional)	p. 16	Duple Rhythmic Chant
Foolin' Around (K. Guilmartin)	p. 28	Duple / Minor & Major / Instrumental
Goodbye, So Long, Farewell (K. Guilmartin)	p. 40	Triple / Major
Hello Song (K. Guilmartin)	p. 13	Duple / Major
Here Is the Beehive (Traditional)	p. 31	Triple Rhythmic Chant
John the Rabbit (Traditional)	p. 25	Duple / Major
Mariá Isabel (Traditional Spanish Folksong)	p. 35	Duple / Major
Ridin' in the Car (K. Guilmartin)	p. 22	Duple / Major
She Sells Sea Shells (K. Guilmartin)	p. 23	Duple / Implied Dorian on D
Sleepyhead (Lyn Ransom)	p. 39	Duple / Major
Stick Dance (K. Guilmartin)	p. 26	Unusual Meter (5/4) / Various Implied Tonalities (Lydian) and some Blues
Su La Li (Bonnie Light)	p. 27	Duple / Minor
The Sad Little Puppy (K. Guilmartin)	p. 21	Duple / Minor
The Train Song (Art Levinowitz)	p. 17	Duple / Major (Vocal Harmony Parts)
Trot, Old Joe (Traditional)	p. 32	Duple / Major

Music Together: Summer Songs 3

Guilmartin, K.K. & Levinowitz, L.M. (2002). *Music together: Summer songs 3*. Princeton, NJ: Music Together LLC. www.musictogether.com.

Contents

Song	Page	Description
All the Pretty Little Horses (Traditional)	p. 27	Duple / Minor (Aeolian or Natural)
Apples and Cherries (Traditional)	p. 23	Duple / Major / Tonal Round
Baa, Baa, Little Star (K. Guilmartin)	p. 28	Duple / Major / Instrumental Play Along
Goodbye, So Long, Farewell (K. Guilmartin)	p. 42	Triple / Major
Hello Song (K. Guilmartin)	p. 13	Duple / Major
Here is a Bunny (Traditional)	p. 33	Triple Rhythm Chant
Hey, Ho, Nobody Home (Traditional)	p. 26	Duple (Swing Rhythm) / Minor
I Had a Little Frog (Traditional)	p. 14	Duple Rhythm Chant
Marching and Drumming (American Civil War Melody)	p. 18	Triple / Natural Minor
Me, You, and We (K. Guilmartin)	p. 15	Duple / Major
My Ball (L. Levinowitz)	p. 25	Unusual Meter (7/8) Rhythmic Chant
Obwisana (Traditional Ghana)	p. 17	Duple / Major
Old King Cole (K. Guilmartin)	p. 35	Duple / Natural Minor
Pussycat (J. Kuhns)	p. 21	Mixed Triple / Phrygian on E
Russian Folk Song (Traditional)	p. 41	Duple / Major
Sailing Song (L. Levinowitz)	p. 19	Triple / Mixolydian on D
See the Pony Galloping (Traditional)	p. 22	Triple / Major
Shake Those 'Simmons Down (Traditional)	p. 40	Duple / Major
Singin' Every Day (K. Guilmartin, South African Melody)	p. 39	Duple / Major
There's a Little Wheel a-Turnin' (Traditional)	p. 36	Duple / Major
Tingalayo (Traditional Spanish)	p. 37	Duple / Major

Music Together: Babies

Guilmartin, K.K. & Levinowitz, L.M. (2002). *Music together: Babies*. Princeton, NJ: Music Together LLC. www.musictogether.com.

Contents

All the Pretty Little Horses (Traditional)	p. 33	Duple / Minor (Aeolian or Natural)
Allee Galloo (Traditional)	p. 39	Triple / Major
Bela Boya (Traditional Bulgarian Folksong)	p. 30	Unusual Meter (7/8) / Implied Dorian Tonality
Breezes (K. Guilmartin)	p. 27	Triple / Mixolydian on D
Dee Da Dum (K. Guilmartin)	p. 23	Duple / Major / Jazz Style
Eensy, Weensy Spider (Traditional American)	p. 25	Triple (or Compound Duple) / Major
Every Day (K. Guilmartin)	p. 22	Combined (Duple with Triplets) / Rhythm Activity
Fireworks (L. Levinowitz)	p. 26	Triple Rhythmic Chant
Goodbye, So Long, Farewell (K. Guilmartin)	p. 52	Triple / Major
Hello Song (K. Guilmartin)	p. 19	Duple / Major
Here Is the Beehive (Traditional)	p. 41	Triple Rhythmic Chant
Hey Ya Na (Traditional Native American—Apache)	p. 45	Duple / Natural Minor
Mary Wore a Red Dress (Traditional)	p. 50	Duple / Major
Merry-Go Round (Lynn Lobban)	p. 40	Triple / Minor
My Bonnie (H. J. Fulmer)	p. 51	Triple / Major
Obwisana (Traditional Ghana)	p. 43	Duple / Major
Simple Gifts (Traditional)	p. 34	Duple / Major / Instrumental Play Along
Sneakin' 'Round the Room (K. Guilmartin)	p. 49	Duple / Minor (can be varied for Triple)
Sweet Potato (Traditional Afro-American Folksong)	p. 29	Duple / Major
There's a Little Wheel a-Turnin' (Traditional)	p. 31	Duple / Major
Tingalayo (Traditional Spanish)	p. 32	Duple / Major
To Market (Traditional & K. Guilmartin)	p. 44	Triple Rhythm Chant
Trot to Grandma's House (Traditional)	p. 21	Duple / Major
Who's That? (Traditional)	p. 37	Duple / Major
William Tell's Ride (Rossini, arr. L. Ransom & K. Guilmartin)	p. 47	Duple / Major and Minor

Music Together: Family Favorites Songbook for Teachers

Guilmartin, K.K. & Levinowitz, L.M. (2009). *Music together: Family favorites songbook for teachers: Bringing harmony home*. Princeton, NJ: Music Together LLC. www.musictogether.com. ISBN: 978-0-615-32865-2.

Contents

Allee Galloo (Traditional)	p. 88	Triple / Major
Biddy Biddy (Traditional)	p. 26	Duple / Major
Dancing With Teddy (K. Guilmartin)	p. 84	Triple / Major
Goin' For Coffee (K. Guilmartin)	p. 70	Duple / Blues on C / Instrumental Play Along
Goodbye, So Long, Farewell (K. Guilmartin)	p. 96	Triple / Major
Hello Song (K. Guilmartin)	p. 22	Duple / Major
I've Been Working on the Railroad (Traditional)	p. 80	Duple / Major
John the Rabbit (Traditional)	p. 54	Duple / Major
May All Children (K. Guilmartin)	p. 92	Multi-Metric (2/4, 3/4, 4/4) / Major
Mississippi Cats (K. Guilmartin)	p. 62	Duple Rhythmic Chant
Obwisana (Traditional Ghana)	p. 76	Duple / Major
One Little Owl (Traditional)	p. 66	Duple / Minor
Palo, Palo (Traditional Dominican Republic)	p. 50	Duple / Major
Playin' in the Kitchen (K. Guilmartin)	p. 46	Duple Rhythmic Chant and Major Tonal Singing
Ridin' in the Car (K. Guilmartin)	p. 34	Duple / Major
She Sells Sea Shells (K. Guilmartin)	p. 42	Duple / Implied Dorian on D
Spin and Stop (L. Levinowitz)	p. 58	Triple Minor
Splishing and Splashing (K. Guilmartin)	p. 30	Duple with Triplets / Rhythmic Chant
Stick Tune (K. Guilmartin)	p. 38	Duple / D Mixolydian

Preschoolers Music Play Index

Music Play: Book 1

Valerio, W., Reynolds, A., Bolton, B., Taggart, C., & Gordon, E. (2000). *Music play: Book 1: The early childhood music curriculum guide for parents, teachers and caregivers.* Chicago, IL: GIA Publications, Inc. Item #G-J236. ISBN: 1-57999-027-4.

The *Music Play* guide includes 57 songs and rhythm chants in a variety of tonalities and meters and over 200 music and movement activities designed to assist you in organizing sequential music and movement experiences for newborn and young children. Each of the songs and rhythm chants found in the guide is recorded on the accompanying compact disc or cassette.

Valerio, W., Reynolds, A., Bolton, B., Taggart, C., & Gordon, E. (1998). *Music play: CD: The early childhood music curriculum guide for parents, teachers and caregivers.* Chicago, IL: GIA Publications, Inc. Item #CD-426.

The beautiful full-color book and CD set includes photos of children engaged in music activities. The book includes notation and lesson plans adapted to the individual needs of each child, as well as a complete introduction to how young children learn when they learn music.

Contents

Songs Without Words (sing with tonal neutral syllable "bum") .... pp. 49-76

"Ring the Bells" ....p. 50		Major / Duple
Acculturation Tonal Pattern 1		Major
Imitation Tonal Pattern 1		Major
Imitation Tonal Pattern 2		Major
Assimilation Pattern Activities		
"My Mommy is a Pilot" ....p. 52		Major / Duple
Acculturation Tonal Pattern 1		Major
Imitation Tonal Pattern 1		Major
Imitation Tonal Pattern 2		Major
Assimilation Pattern Activities		
"Bumble Bee" ....p. 54		Major / Multi-Metric (Unusual Paired 5/8 & Triple)
Acculturation Tonal Pattern 1		Major
Imitation Tonal Pattern 1		Major
Imitation Tonal Pattern 2		Major
Assimilation Pattern Activities		

Song	Page	Tonality / Meter
"I Saw a Dinosaur"	p. 56	Major / Duple
(Acculturation, Imitation, Assimilation activities continue with each song)		
"Winter Day"	p. 58	Harmonic Minor / Unusual Paired (5/8)
"The Sled"	p. 60	Harmonic Minor / Triple / ABA Form
"Pennsylvania Dreamin'"	p. 62	Harmonic Minor / Triple
"Planting Flowers"	p. 64	Melodic Minor / Triple
"Goldfish"	p. 66	Dorian / Triple
"Dancing"	p. 67	Dorian / Duple
"Jumping"	p. 68	Dorian" / Triple
"Ocean Waves"	p. 69	Dorian / Triple
"Country Dance"	p. 70	Mixolydian / Triple
"Red Umbrella"	p. 71	Dorian / Unusual Unpaired (7/8) / Ritardando
"Albany"	p. 72	Mixolydian / Multi-Metric (Triple & Duple)
"Good-bye"	p. 73	Phrygian / Triple
"Stirring Soup"	p. 74	Phrygian / Unusual Paired (5/8)
"Daydreams"	p. 75	Locrian / Duple

Chants Without Words (chant with rhythm neutral syllable "ba") ....pp. 77-98

"Follow Me!"	p. 78	Duple
"Stretch and Bounce"	p. 80	Duple
"Walking With My Mom"	p. 82	Duple / Accent
"Fireworks"	p. 84	Duple / Crescendo / Subito
"Rolling"	p. 86	Triple
"Popsicle"	p. 88	Triple / Crescendo / Decrescendo / Same and Different
"Child Song"	p. 90	Triple
"Snowflake"	p. 92	Harmonic Minor (Recorded accompaniment) / Triple
"Rain"	p. 94	Unusual Paired (5/8) / Timbre Awareness
"Panda"	p. 95	Unusual Paired (5/8)
"Buggy Ride"	p. 96	Unusual Unpaired (7/8) / Accent
"Wild Pony"	p. 97	Unusual Unpaired (7/8) / Accent
"Train Ride"	p. 98	Unusual Unpaired (7/8) / Accent

Songs With Words .... pp. 99-111

"Down By the Station"	p. 100	Major / Duple
"Jeremiah Blow the Fire"	p. 101	Major / Duple
"Roll the Ball Like This"	p. 102	Harmonic Minor / Triple
"My Pony Bill"	p. 103	Harmonic Minor / Triple
"Ni, Nah, Noh"	p. 104	Aeolian / Triple / Ritardando / Same and Different
"Bushes and Briars"	p. 105	Dorian / Triple / Same and Different
"To the Window"	p. 106	Dorian or Aeolian / Unusual Paired (5/8)
"Swinging"	p. 107	Mixolydian / Triple
"Jerry Hall"	p. 108	Mixolydian / Unusual Paired (5/8)
"The Wind"	p. 109	Lydian / Triple
"Poor Bengy"	p. 110	Phrygian / Duple
"North and South"	p. 111	Locrian / Duple

Chants With Words .... pp. 112-124

"My Mother, Your Mother"	p. 113	Duple
"Popcorn"	p. 114	Duple
"Go and Stop"	p. 115	Duple
"Sidewalk Talk"	p. 116	Duple
"This Little Piggy"	p. 117	Triple
"Clackety Clack"	p. 118	Triple
"Hickety Pickety Bumble Bee"	p. 119	Triple
"Here is the Beehive"	p. 120	Triple / Tempo (Quick and Slow)
"Jump Over the Ocean"	p. 121	Triple
"Flop"	p. 122	Unusual Unpaired (7/8)
"In the Tub"	p. 123	Unusual Unpaired (7/8)
"Hop and Stop"	p. 124	Multi-Metric (Unusual Paired 5/8 & Triple)

Preschoolers Nichol's Worth Books Index

A Nichol's Worth
Volumes 1, 2, 3, & 4

Nichol, Doug (1975). *A Nichol's worth. Volumes 1 & 2 (1975). Volumes 3 & 4 (1978).* Buffalo, NY: Tometic Associates LTD. Reprinted with permission. University Park, PA: The Pennsylvania State University Bookstore.

A collection of witty, folk-like songs in four volumes, featuring duple, triple, and multi-metric combined meters; in Major, Minor, Dorian, Mixolydian, Phrygian, Lydian, and multi-tonal modes; and in vocal textures of unison, combinable songs, partner songs, ostinatos, countermelodies, and rounds.

Contents

A Nichol's Worth, Volume I .... pp. 1-52

"Acceptance"	p. 42	Combined Meter (Duple with Triplets) / Minor / Unison
"Boy I'm Gonna Get Stuffed With Food"	p. 12	Triple / Dorian / Unison
"Changeable Chug-a-lug"	p. 50	Duple / Triple / Major / Combinable
"Do You Believe It?"	p. 26	Duple / Major / Partner
"Fireman, Fireman"	p. 5	Duple / Minor / Ostinato
"Freedom"	p. 32	Duple / Major / Countermelody
"Grandma Has a Habit"	p. 2	Triple / Mixolydian / Countermelody
"The Grasshopper and the Elephant"	p. 9	Duple / Phrygian / Unison
"Happiness is Giving"	p. 15	Duple / Mixolydian / Partner
"Hot Dog"	p. 4	Unusual Meter (5/8) / Major / Unison
"I Don't Believe It"	p. 27	Duple / Major / Partner
"I'm Your Friend"	p. 14	Duple / Mixolydian / Partner
"I Want to Be Lonely"	p. 22	Duple / Major / Unison
"I Would Give You the World"	p. 36	Triple / Major / Unison
"Let's Make It Christmas All the Time"	p. 16	Duple / Major / Countermelodies
"Look For the Bright Side"	p. 38	Duple / Major / Combinable
"Love Would Increase"	p. 44	Duple / Dorian / Countermelodies
"New Shoes"	p. 6	Duple / Major / Unison

"Nobody Cares" .... p. 40   Duple / Lydian / Countermelodies

"One of These Days" .... p. 35   Unusual (6/8 with Duple & Triple) / Mixolydian / Round

"Peas" .... p. 1   Triple / Lydian / Unison

"The Secret" .... p. 30   Duple / Minor / Unison

"The Squirrel" .... p. 8   Triple / Phrygian / Unison

"There Won't Be Any to Save" .... p. 24   Duple / Major / Unison

"Time" .... p. 46   Duple / Major / Countermelody

"What Am I?" .... p. 28   Duple / Mixolydian / Ostinato

"When I'm Thinking of You" .... p. 19   Duple / Major / Combinable

"Where In the World Did I Put My Mittens?" ..... p. 10   Duple / Major / Unison

"Who Says?" .... p. 20   Duple / Mixolydian / Unison

A Nichol's Worth, Volume II .... pp. 1-52

"Autumn" .... p. 22   Triple / Minor & Dorian / Countermelody

"Bangity Wangity Wapsy Boom" .... p. 1   Triple / Major / Unison

"Boy, I Wish I Were Ninety Feet Tall" .... p. 2   Triple / Dorian / Unison

"Come On You People" .... p. 51   Duple / Major / Round

"Chug-a-lug Choo Choo" .... p. 29   Unusual (5/8) / Major / Round

"The Eagle" .... p. 50   Duple / Minor / Unison

"Eletelephony" .... p. 3   Duple / Mixolydian / Unison

"Funny Shape" .... p. 20   Triple / Lydian / Countermelodies

"Give a Little Love" .... p. 30   Duple / Major / Combinable

"H-A-double P-I-N-E-double S" .... p. 8   Duple / Major / Unison

"The Hootchy Kootchy Dance" .... p. 6   Duple / Mixolydian / Countermelodies

"I Do Better When I Try My Best" .... p. 40   Duple / Major / Countermelody

"I'm Tired of Bein' Busy" .... p. 42   Duple / Major / Unison

"It's Not Too Bad to Be Me" .... p. 46   Duple / Lydian / Combinable

"Living Spring" .... p. 10   Combined (Duple with Triplets) / Major / Round

"Oh, It's Great to Be Living This Morning" .... p. 34   Duple / Major / Combinable

"The Old Swamp Band" .... p. 26   Duple / Major / Unison

"Over" .... p. 39   Duple / Major / Unison

"People Who Need Your Help" .... p. 16   Duple / Major / Countermelodies

"Sam, Sam, the Butcher Man" .... p. 9   Duple / Lydian / Ostinatos

"Snow" .... p. 44   Triple / Major / Combinable

"Summer Is"	p. 11	Triple / Mixolydian / Round
"The Summer's Near"	p. 48	Duple / Minor / Unison
"Three Limericks"	p. 12	Triple / Mixolydian / Partner
"Turkey Struttin' 'Round"	p. 4	Duple / Mixolydian / Unison
"What Would the World Be Like Without Music?"	p. 14	Duple / Major / Combinable
"The Whistle"	p. 19	Duple / Major / Unison
"You Make Me Glad That I Know You"	p. 36	Duple / Major / Unison

A Nichol's Worth, Volume III ....pp. 1-31

"Be Thankful For Love"	p. 28	Duple / Major / Unison
"Cold Wind of Winter"	p. 8	Duple / Major / Unison
"Dancing Bear"	p. 13	Duple / Major / Unison
"Don't Be A Slob"	p. 9	Combined (Duple & Triple) / Lydian / Unison
"Do You Ever?"	p. 14	Triple / Major / Unison
"Elephants, Monkeys, and Leopards"	p. 5	Triple / Major / Combinable
"Farm, Farm, Farm, Farm"	p. 2	Duple / Major / Combinable
"The Grasswalker"	p. 22	Unusual (5/8) / Major / Combinable
"Gus"	p. 3	Triple / Dorian / Unison
"Had A Little Thought"	p. 20	Duple / Major / Partner
"I Love A Melody"	p. 21	Duple / Major / Partner
"It's All Pretend"	p. 10	Triple / Minor / Unison
"I Want To Be A Circus Clown"	p. 15	Triple / Mixolydian / Unison
"March"	p. 1	Duple / Major / Combinable
"The Middle of the Night"	p. 6	Duple / Phrygian / Unison
"Misery To A Kid"	p. 30	Duple / Major / Unison
"My Aminal"	p. 29	Duple / Minor / Unison
"My Secret Tree"	p. 24	Duple / Major / Unison
"Oh, I'll Build A Snowman"	p. 18	Triple / Minor / Partner
"Oh, Moe Is We"	p. 26	Duple / Major / Unison
"Old Folks"	p. 12	Duple / Major / Combinable
"Pancakes"	p. 25	Duple / Major / Unison
"Shiver"	p. 7	Duple / Major / Unison
"Song For Any Season"	p. 16	Duple / Mixolydian & Dorian / Countermelody
"Take A Look at Your Life"	p. 11	Unusual (7/8) / Major / Round
"We Share the World Together"	p. 4	Duple / Major / Combinable
"Why Don't They Feel Like Me"	p. 19	Triple / Minor / Partner

A Nichol's Worth, Volume IV ....pp. 1-39

"A Favorite Thing to Me"	p. 24	Duple / Major / Unison

"April Rain"	p. 16	Triple / Phrygian / Round
"Children Are Laughing"	p. 32	Duple / Major / Unison
"Come On and Laugh With Me"	p. 19	Duple / Major / Partner
"The Eefin' Song"	p. 28	Duple / Minor / Combinable
"February"	p. 1	Duple / Major / Unison
"I Can Feel the Beauty"	p. 17	Duple / Major / Unison
"I'd Like to Roller Skate on the Moon"	p. 38	Duple / Major / Unison
"I'm So Unhappy"	p. 18	Duple / Major / Partner
"It's Snowing"	p. 4	Triple / Major / Partner
"January"	p. 6	Duple / Major / Combinable
"Johnson Boys"	p. 30	Duple / Major / Countermelody
"Just Give Me a Cloudy Day"	p. 2	Duple / Major / Unison
"Let Me Be"	p. 27	Triple / Lydian / Countermelody
"Let's Play in the Snow"	p. 4	Triple / Major / Partner
"Magic Land"	p. 20	Duple / Major / Combinable
"Monkey Business"	p. 13	Duple / Mixolydian / Round
"My Little Friend"	p. 34	Duple / Major / Unison
"Oh, Yeah?"	p. 5	Triple / Dorian / Unison
"Rain"	p. 26	Triple / Major / Combinable
"Smile and Be Yourself"	p. 14	Duple / Major / Countermelody
"There Were Some Times"	p. 36	Duple / Major / Unison
"Things Are For Things"	p. 25	Unusual (Multi-Metric) / Major / Unison
"We Are Together"	p. 8	Duple / Major / Unison
"You'll Sound As Weird As Me"	p. 25	Triple / Multi-Tonal / Unison
"You Ought To"	p. 12	Triple / Minor / Unison
"You're As Good As All of the Rest"	p. 10	Triple / Dorian / Unison

Preschoolers Movement with Instrumental Music

The Book of Movement Exploration: Can You Move Like This?

Feierabend, J., & Kahan, J. (2003). *The book of movement exploration: Can you move like this?* Chicago, IL: GIA Publications, Inc. ISBN 1-57999-264-1.

Feierabend, J. (2110). *First steps in classical music: Keeping the beat! (Compiled by John Feierabend)*. Chicago, IL: GIA Publications, Inc. CD#: CD-493

Book Contents

Theme 1: Awareness of Body Parts & Whole ....pp. 11-16

    1.1 Whole Body Movement .... p. 12
    1.2 Isolated Body Parts .... p. 13
    1.3 Leading with a Part .... p. 16
    1.4 Initiating with a Part .... p. 16

Theme 2: Awareness of Time ....pp. 17-18

    2.1 Quick and Slow Movement .... p. 18
    2.2 Clock Time .... p. 18

Theme 3: Awareness of Space ....pp. 21-28

    3.1 Personal Space and General Space .... p. 22
    3.2 Direct / Indirect Pathway (Straight / Twisted) .... p. 22
    3.3 Inward Movement (Narrow) .... p. 24
    3.4 Outward Movement (Wide) .... p. 25
    3.5 Direction of Movement .... p. 27
    3.6 Distance of Movement .... p. 28

Theme 4: Awareness of Levels ....pp. 21-32

    4.1 High / Middle / Low .... p. 32

Theme 5: Awareness of Weight .... pp. 35-37

    5.1 Heavy / Light .... p. 36
    5.2 Strong / Gentle .... p. 37
    5.3 Tense / Relaxed .... p. 37

Theme 6: Awareness of Locomotion .... p. 49

Theme 7: Awareness of Flow .... pp. 43-46

    7.1 Sudden / Sustained .... p. 44
    7.2 Sequential / Simultaneous .... p. 45
    7.3 Bound / Free .... p. 46

Theme 8: Awareness of Shape .... pp. 49-50

    8.1 Becoming Shapes .... p. 50

Theme 9: Awareness of Others .... pp. 53-57

    9.1 Partners .... p. 54
    9.2 Groups .... p. 57

Theme 10: Student Created Movement .... pp. 59-63

    10.1 Representative Movement .... p. 60
    10.2 Non-Representative Movement .... p. 63

CD Contents and Music Concepts

Excerpt time lengths range from 1:09 to 2:55:

1. Concerto No. 10 in C Major (Arcangelo Corelli)......... Major / Duple / Tempo = MM132

2. Concerto No. 11 in Bb Flat Major: *Allemanda, Allegro* (Arcangelo Corelli)
.... Major / Duple / Tempo = MM130

3. Concerto No. 12 in F Major (Arcangelo Corelli)
.... Major / Duple Compound / Tempo = MM132

4. Concert in F Major: *Giga, Allegro* (Arcangelo Corelli)
.... Major / Triple / Tempo = MM126

5. Gloria in D, RV 589: *Domini Fili* (Antonio Vivaldi)
.... Major / Triple / Tempo = MM126

6. Suite and Dances: *Premier et deuxiéme contredanse* (Jean-Philip Rameau)
.... Major / Duple / Tempo = MM130

7. Suite No. 3 in D, BWV 1068: *Gigue* (J.S. Bach)
.... Major / Duple Compound / Tempo = MM120

8. Suite No. 4 in D, BWV 1069: *Gavotte* (J. S. Bach)
.... Major / Duple / Tempo = MM136

9. Suite No. 4 in D, BWV 1069: *Rejouissance* (J. S. Bach)
.... Major / Duple / Tempo = MM126

10. Suite No. 2 in b minor, BWV 1067: *Bourée I and II* (J. S. Bach)
.... Minor / Duple / Tempo = MM120

11. Suite No. 2 in b minor, BWV 1067: *Minuet* (J. S. Bach)
.... Minor / Triple / Tempo = MM132

12. Suite No. 2 in b minor, BWV 1067: Badinerie (J. S. Bach)
.... Minor / Duple / Tempo = MM126

13. Magnificat: Et exsultavit (J. S. Bach) .... Major / Triple / Tempo = MM122

14. Water Music: Allegro: (Gigue) (George Frideric Handel)
.... Major / Duple Compound / Tempo = MM136

15. Fireworks Music: Minuet II (George Frideric Handel)
.... Major / Triple / Tempo = MM132

16. Water Music: Minuet (George Frideric Handel) .... Major / Triple / Tempo = MM124

17. Concerto grosso in D Major, Op. 1, No. 5: *Allegro* (Pietro Locatelli)
.... Major / Duple / Tempo = MM136

18. Concerto grosso in D Major, Op. 1, No. 9: *Allegro* (Pietro Locatelli)
.... Major / Triple / Tempo = MM136

19. Eine kliene Nachtmusik, K. 525: *Allegro* (Wolfgang Amadeus Mozart)
.... Major / Duple / Tempo = MM132

20. Eine kliene Nachtmusik, K. 525: *Rondo, Allegro* (Wolfgang Amadeus Mozart)
.... Major / Duple / Tempo = MM120

21. Symphony No. 40 in g minor, K. 550: *Allegro assai* (Wolfgang Amadeus Mozart)
.... Major / Duple / Tempo = MM126

22. Ballet Music from Faust: *Allegretto* (Charles Gounod)
.... Minor / Duple / Tempo = MM120

23. Gaîté Parisienne: Overture (Jacques Offenbach)..... Major / Duple / Tempo = MM126

24. Gaîté Parisienne: *Guadrille* and *Allegro* (Jacques Offenbach)
.... Major / Duple / Tempo = MM120

25. Gaîté Parisienne: *Allegro* and *Allegro* (Jacques Offenbach)
.... Major / Duple / Tempo = MM136

26. Hungarian Dances: No. 18 (Johannes Brahms)........ Minor / Duple / Tempo = MM136

27. Swan Lake: Spanish Dance (Peter Ilyich Tchaikovsky)
.... Major / Triple / Tempo = MM124

28. The Nutcracker: Overture (Peter Ilyich Tchaikovsky)
....Major / Duple / Tempo = MM128

29. Ancient Airs and Dances: Suite No. 1: Baletto detto "Il Conte Orlando" (Ottorino Respighi) ....Major / Duple / Tempo = MM126

30. Ancient Airs and Dances: Suite No. 2: Laura Soave (Ottorino Respighi)
....Major / Duple / Tempo = MM126

31. Háry János Suite: Viennese Musical Clock (Zoltan Kodaly)
....Major / Duple / Tempo = MM128

32. Pulcinella Suite: *Allegro* (Igor Stravinsky) ....Major / Duple / Tempo = MM126

33. Symphony No. 1 in D Major: Gavotte: *Non troppo allegro* (Sergei Prokofiev)
....Major / Duple / Tempo = MM120

34. Rodeo: Hoe-Down (Aaron Copeland) ....Major / Duple / Tempo = MM128

35. Romeo and Juliet: Preparation for the Ball (Dmitry Kabalevsky)
....Major / Duple / Tempo = MM126

36. The Comedians: Epilogue (Dmitry Kabalevsky) ....Major / Duple / Tempo = MM126

Notes for
BOOK 3: PRESCHOOLERS

www.ingramcontent.com/pod-product-compliance
Lightning Source LLC
Chambersburg PA
CBHW080539300426
44111CB00017B/2802